ADVANCE PRAISE FOR FINDING WORK AFTER 40

'This book explodes myths surrounding older workers and – by giving a range of practical strategies – boosts confidence for those career changers who worry that their date of birth puts them out of the race.'

John Lees, author of How To Get A Job You'll Love
(McGraw-Hill)

'This is a timely book. From the age of 40 onwards, age-related disadvantage is a subtle force undermining employability and confidence for individuals seeking work. A history of low investment in skills and versatility often blights their job prospects. Research shows convincingly that they bring tremendous added value but bizarrely, employers fail to tap the mid-life talent pool when filling vacancies. So mid-life job seekers need to maximise their own marketability, understand their strengths, and correct their weaknesses. They must network like hell and adopt clever job search strategies. *Finding Work After 40* takes these elements apart and sets the mid-life job seeker on the right road. Hopefully, if people read this we will hear fewer stories of desperate individuals making a thousand applications and receiving no job offers.'

Chris Ball, Chief Executive,
TAEN (The Age and Employment Network)

'This book makes a serious step in protecting one of society's major assets, the value of its mature work-force. Everyone 'doing' corporate social responsibility (an increasing number daily) should read this book and use it. The authors have achieved the difficult balance between being authoritative, which they undoubtedly are, and being approachable enough for all who read the book to feel that it is written for them. The supporting evidence and illustrations are so constructed as to enhance understanding which is essential in building confidence and deep conviction in one's abilities.'

Professor Alan Richardson, Chair of Science in Enterprise,
The Royal Institution of Great Britain

FINDING WORK AFTER 40

FINDING WORK AFTER 40

Proven Strategies for Managers and Professionals

Robin McKay Bell and Liam Mifsud

A & C Black • London

First published in Great Britain 2011

A & C Black, an imprint of Bloomsbury Publishing Plc
36 Soho Square, London W1D 3QY

A CIP record for this book is available from the British Library.

ISBN: 978-1-4081-3125-1

This book is produced using paper that is made from wood grown in managed, sustainable forests. It is natural, renewable and recyclable. The logging and manufacturing processes conform to the environmental regulations of the country of origin.

Design by Fiona Pike, Pike Design, Winchester
Typeset by Saxon Graphics Ltd, Derby
Printed in the United Kingdom by Martins The Printers, Berwick-upon-Tweed

TABLE OF CONTENTS

SECTION FOUR
Move Forward: Get a Job

SECTION FIVE
Move Forward: Self-Employment

INTRODUCTION

Many career books cover the topics of unemployment and re-entry into the workforce. This one is different because it's specifically for managers and professionals aged 40 to 65, the 'forgotten workforce', the one that is assumed to be okay but, in reality, is much in need of advice and assistance when things go wrong. Age discrimination often stands in the way of re-employment, and so older workers must take a different approach when tackling the problem. For many readers, especially those in their 50s or 60s, 40 may seem a bit young to be called 'older', but our experience is that in some sectors (such as IT) being over 40 is a factor that counts against applicants. It's also the age at which many people will begin to re-examine their career and life goals, with an eye to improving their situation. As well as helping those who have been made redundant find a new job, the book is designed as a practical guide to mid-life career change. It's called *Finding* **Work** *After 40* because a job (in the traditional sense) may not be the solution to your problem; work in the form of self-employment or a portfolio career are options to consider. So if you have been made redundant or you think it's about to happen, if you're contemplating a fresh start, or if you are one of several million older workers who cannot afford retirement, this book is for you.

OUR MOTTO

We describe our concept in seven words: *'Know yourself, sell yourself, network like crazy'*. That summarises our approach to work search. If you're able to do those three things well, your chances of getting back into work (or changing career) are vastly improved. We explain each one thoroughly, and provide methods and exercises that help you to improve in areas where you are lacking. You'll learn how to:

- carry out a productive skills audit so you can discover and understand the value of your 'transferable' and 'motivated' skills *(know yourself)*;
- describe yourself persuasively in professional and social circumstances, in letters and CVs, as well as in interviews *(sell yourself)*;
- network effectively to acquire, develop and maintain useful contacts *(network like crazy)*.

HOW THE BOOK WORKS

In Section One we tell you how to deal with 'the seven elephants in the room' – the age barriers that stand between you and the work you want. We also explain how our work culture evolved to discriminate against older workers, and we discuss briefly what changes the future may bring. If you've been made redundant, Chapter 2 offers advice on how to cope with your situation.

Section Two takes you through an effective assessment of your skills and abilities. A key message in this book is that you must know your strengths to sell yourself effectively. We caution against blindly sending out CVs and completing online applications, because self-knowledge is your competitive advantage. You'll need to look at your options, examine the market, and take a reality check. Then you will be asked to make a decision and create a forward plan from three basic choices: a job; self-employment; or a combination of both in a portfolio career.

In Section Three we show you how to improve your network: the essential skill that must be developed in order to succeed. The section includes a chapter on upgrading your skills. Section Four details methods of finding and getting a job; Section Five explores various types of self-employment and tells you how to get started.

Our 'Work Funnel' diagram illustrates how the book is structured from Chapter 4 onwards, directing the 'flow' of your efforts towards a positive outcome. You'll notice that it reappears in some chapters, as a reminder of where you are located in reference to the funnel.

THE WORK FUNNEL

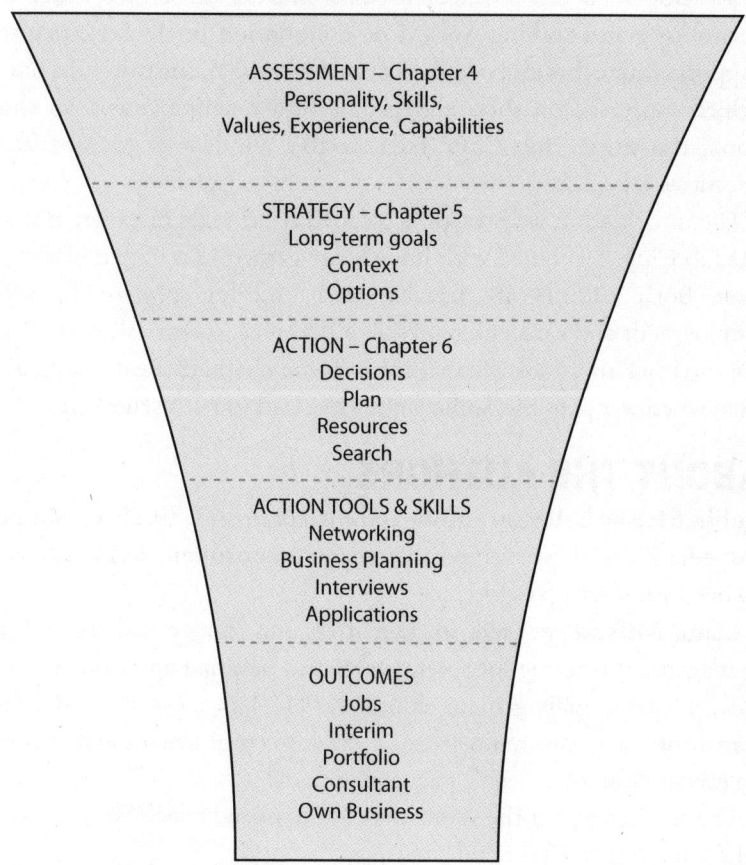

ASSESSMENT – Chapter 4
Personality, Skills,
Values, Experience, Capabilities

STRATEGY – Chapter 5
Long-term goals
Context
Options

ACTION – Chapter 6
Decisions
Plan
Resources
Search

ACTION TOOLS & SKILLS
Networking
Business Planning
Interviews
Applications

OUTCOMES
Jobs
Interim
Portfolio
Consultant
Own Business

WHY WE'RE SPECIAL

This is a practical book, based on real-life experience. We've detailed successful techniques developed by a network of job clubs. As part of the network, the Windsor & Maidenhead Executive Job Club was created in 2005 to assist white-collar workers over the age of 45 in their efforts to re-enter the workforce. Initially supported by the Branshaw Foundation Limited (and now by the Foundation for Jobseekers) the club is run by volunteers; it hosts weekly meetings featuring presentations that cover every aspect of job search and mid-life career change. It isn't a passive operation; members are encouraged to develop their self-promotion skills, and to assist each other in networking and seeking work. The Foundation for Jobseekers also supports four other clubs in Berkshire. Since 2005, the five clubs have helped more than a thousand people find re-employment. In this book, the words 'Job Club' refer to the Windsor & Maidenhead Executive Job Club.

The information we present is gleaned from years of experience at the Job Club, combined with knowledge gained in our own working lives. Both authors are familiar with mid-life job search, self-employment and career change. All of the 'success stories' are true, as are the brief anecdotes we include in some chapters. Real names are used whenever possible; sometimes we've had to use pseudonyms.

ABOUT THE AUTHORS

Robin McKay Bell is an author and entrepreneur with a background in media. He has been an interim manager, a consultant and a business owner with start-up experience.

Liam Mifsud worked in executive and career coaching and management training for several years and he's had an associate role with a career management company. He has recently made the transition back into mainstream corporate employment and is now an executive at a renewable energy company.

The authors met at the Windsor & Maidenhead Executive Job Club, where Liam is co-Chair and a trustee.

ACKNOWLEDGEMENTS

The book was inspired by thousands of men and women who attended Job Club meetings. Many people made a contribution. Isabella Kerr gave us support and encouragement and she contributed her expertise on age and employment. Brian Murphy (Job Club co-Chair) and volunteers Hugh Gordon, Alison Fair and Sanda Ionescu commented constructively on the content, as did Alan Richardson. We are grateful to Dr Chris Ball and Professor Stephen McNair for providing valuable input on the age issue. Thanks are due to Mike Taylor, Paul Lower,

Katie Ledger and Adrian Bourne for their comments on chapters in the self-employment section. Ben Makins helped us with suggestions for public sector workers. Those who contributed their personal stories deserve a special thank-you: John McGee, Trevor Gent, Mike Carr, Anne Burchett, Graham Stephens, Natalie Mclellan, Jane Evans, Alan Saxon, Ben Makins, Matt Williams, Paul Lower, William Priest and Judith Watts. Thanks also to those who told us their stories but preferred to remain anonymous.

Very special thanks are due to Mark Parker for contributing the illustrations.

Our wives and families deserve the highest praise for their patient understanding when 'having to work on the book' was an excuse not to do so many things. Finally, we'd like to acknowledge each other – neither of us could have done this alone.

DEDICATION

Finding Work After 40 is dedicated to all those out-of-work middle-aged men and women who think there is no end in sight to their search for employment. As the success stories in this book illustrate, there is. We hope that we've provided you with the tools to reflect on your capabilities, the guidance to present them powerfully, and the inspiration to keep going until you find the work you want.

1

Get Over It:
Age and Redundancy

THE AGE FACTOR 1

Surveys show that many employers value older workers because they are reliable, dependable, loyal, skilful, and able to draw on a wealth of life experiences that can be applied to their work[1]. Rates of short-term absenteeism are lower and retention rates are higher. In other words: older workers make excellent employees. And yet the 50-plus age group has the highest incidence of long-term unemployment[2], those over 45 find it difficult to get re-employed, and in some sectors it can be hard to find work after 40. Clearly there are age-related obstacles to be overcome.

SEVEN ELEPHANTS IN THE ROOM

Isabella Kerr, Project Manager at the Foundation for Jobseekers, offers some valuable words of advice. She says that:

> 'Older workers need to be pragmatic and positive with the world as it is. It's necessary to accept that age stereotypes exist and then operate intelligently in order to factor in the objections that an employer may have. Analyse them and find ways to work with them.'[3]

Her suggestion is to seed your responses with information that runs counter to those objections. She also says, 'If these objections have not been addressed in the interview, then the interview hasn't been successful.'

At the Job Club, we've defined seven 'elephants in the room': the age stereotypes and objections that are commonly held by employers, which are sitting there and being ignored, but influencing the decision-makers. The challenge is to acknowledge and understand each elephant and then respond to the stereotype in a positive way. We'll show you how it's done.

1. An older person won't work for a younger manager or with a younger team

The converse is also true: a younger manager or team won't want an older person because they won't fit with the culture.

This is a big elephant. In some interviews it may be the only one. The best-qualified candidate can lose the role because a younger man or woman doesn't want an older person working beneath them. It makes them uncomfortable. They just can't get their heads around having someone nearly as old as their mum or dad answering and reporting to them. It feels unnatural. The boss is usually the oldest one on the team, or they may manage several teams. The owner of the company, or the chairman, is the senior person in the room. If we examine corporate pyramids, we see older people at the very top and the expectation is that, at a certain age, a person occupies a specific place in the hierarchy. Acceptable age limits are measured against a corporate norm.

Anecdotal evidence suggests corporate recruiters and recruitment agencies perpetuate the problem of age discrimination. Those who do the preliminary screening and the first interview are generally in their 20s or 30s. A 25-year-old will want to select an up-and-coming 30-year-old over someone who is 50. In other words, younger people are discriminating against older people.

To engage with this problem, ask yourself two questions:

'Does success in the role mean being able to fit in with a young team?' and 'Will success be the result of experience and technical skills?'

If the team is young, then your age is a factor, and for a good reason. But if the job requires experience and skills that you have, then age should not be a problem. Remember these questions can be voiced at an interview. It's a way of exposing the truth about the situation and the corporate culture.

If you're fortunate, you'll be able to appeal to a manager's belief in the value of an older worker (see John McGee's story on p.16).

2. An older worker is overqualified

This is a common excuse, when in fact someone may fit the profile of a perfect candidate, except for their age. Some employers will interview an older candidate as part of a box-ticking exercise, with no intention of hiring them. In that event, shake the dirt off your feet and carry on. However, there might be other reasons for an employer saying you have too much experience. They may be worried that you are taking the job as a stopgap, and that you'll leave when you find something better. If that is the case, be honest and admit it. A recruiter who understands your situation may be sympathetic. See Michael's story on p.184. He's an example of someone who was able to convince his employer that he had very good reasons to seek a job for which he was overqualified.

If they're worried about you leaving after a year and asking for redundancy pay, you could offer yourself on a contract basis to eliminate the objection. The message is: bring the objections into the open; discuss them with the recruiter, and negotiate if possible.

We have two other suggestions:

- **Tone down your CV and make it relevant only to the position you're applying for. If your CV is loaded with vast amounts of experience, it's *you* who has told them that you're overqualified.**
- **Accept that in order to stay employed at a level down from your previous position, you will have to keep your opinions to yourself and not be the person who tells everyone how to do it better. Your challenge is to convince a recruiter that this is true.**

3. Older people lack energy

Most of us have to admit that we have less energy now than when we were 21 or 35. It's a biological fact that we slow down as we age. Even with regular exercise, you're likely to be less fit than you were ten years ago. With the exception of golf or snooker, nearly every sport sees its top competitors retire from competition by the age of 40, if not sooner. So there's no point in pretending that your energy levels are as high as they once were. The question is: do they have to be? Young people can waste a lot of energy. A mature person will often accomplish more in the same time frame, because the task is performed more efficiently. In the hare and tortoise story, the tortoise wins because he isn't distracted by every whim of the moment. He stays on track and completes the race with a slow, steady pace. He's smarter than the hare; he knows his limits and works with them to succeed. He has also learned alternative ways of solving problems, and knows people who can help.

To win the contract or get the job, the employer must be convinced that you have the right amount of energy, and that you're able to sustain it. Projecting enthusiasm for the position is a first step. And if you're still able to run a marathon, compete in cycling races or climb a mountain, then drop that into a conversation. If you're not, don't worry. It's the projection of energy – creating a perception of health – that matters.

4. Older workers have health problems

This ties in with energy because everyone knows that health issues can complicate life in middle age. If your health is good, do you *look* healthy? Our mission with this book is to do more than simply advise people to cheer up, lose weight, get a better suit and upgrade their eyeglasses. However, investing in your appearance will demonstrate a positive attitude, which will always count in your favour.

Look at yourself in the mirror. Don't ask your husband, wife, partner or friend about your appearance. They will want to encourage you, and so they're unlikely to tell the honest truth. If you're unemployed, they know you're feeling low about your situation and they'll want to build you up. But what do *you* think? You have to sell yourself in the employment market. In order to be effective you must project confidence and know that you're able to do the job. Does your appearance say you're not looking after yourself? If you think so, then take action. You might need to seek advice.

If you are unhealthy, in that you have a medical condition that would impede your ability to work, then it's not wise to insist on pressing forward, even if there is a financial imperative. Once hired, there is the responsibility to execute your duties. Would extended absences interfere with your ability to perform in the role? And is it fair to deceive an employer?

Keep in mind that, under the Equality Act, employers can't discriminate on health and disability grounds, and they cannot ask questions about your health prior to the job offer stage. Even so, you need to first be honest with yourself and then later be prepared to be truthful with a potential employer about your general health.

5. An older worker has money, so they don't really need the job

Whether or not you've got anything put by for a rainy day, there may be a perception that you have, simply because you're older. Therefore a recruiter may assume you aren't as motivated or as driven as someone younger because, for you, money is not an issue. Ironically, you may need the money *more* than a younger candidate. The mortgage still has to be paid, there's university for the kids, and there may be costs in taking care of an ageing parent.

Countering this prejudice is tricky. Being too needy is always negative, yet appearing to be the opposite can also cost you an opportunity. Mention reasons why you are the best candidate; focus on personal fulfilment, a desire for new challenges and experiences, and your motivation for success, which can include financial rewards or payment for a project completed.

If you sense that this 'elephant' is working against you, see if you can have a quiet word with the most senior person at the interview, or by private communication. Sometimes they will take a kinder view if they know your situation.

6. Older people are not mentally agile

The British and American psychologist Raymond Cattell developed a theory that, broadly speaking, there are two types of intelligence: *fluid* and *crystallised*[4]. They are correlated, in that one does not exist without the other. Fluid intelligence is the capacity to think independently of acquired knowledge to apply logic to problem solving. It includes inductive and deductive reasoning. There is evidence that, as we age, our fluid intelligence wanes. On this basis, young people tend to perceive those who are older as slower and therefore less mentally agile.

Crystallised intelligence is knowledge gained by experience, and it includes verbal skills, general information and the ability to create analogies – it adds up to what we call wisdom. For example, negotiating skills depend more on crystallised intelligence. Evidence shows that crystallised intelligence increases with age, remains stable, and doesn't begin to diminish until after the age of 65[5]. This effect varies greatly, with many people maintaining their crystallised intelligence to an advanced age.

As an excuse for not hiring an older person, this one doesn't have a foundation in science.

7. Older workers can't deal with change

Every stereotype has some basis in fact. Some people in the 40 to 65 age group can't cope with change, so that is what some employers might think about you, perhaps because they already have someone on their staff who is set in their ways. They might also project that characteristic on to every older person they meet. That could fairly be called a prejudice, one that is difficult to fight. It's impossible to know what's in the mind of a recruiter at any given moment.

In reality, mature people are often better than their younger counterparts at dealing with change in the workplace because they've already learned to adapt to variables of every sort. For example, the recent recession is the first one that many younger managers will have seen. Someone in their 40s or 50s will have lived through at least two downturns. Your experience in managing situations through tough times proves you know how to handle changes.

The ability to adapt and be flexible is individual, and is not necessarily age-based. It has more to do with personality than age.

Search your history to find evidence of where you changed in order to achieve new goals.

Leaving the 'elephants' behind, you also will need to manage your expectations.

REMUNERATION

When some people first arrive at the Job Club, they're convinced that, with enough effort, they can return to the same position and the same salary they had before they were made redundant. Surely if someone has been a marketing director on a six-figure salary, then that's what they're worth, isn't it? Our experience has shown that most people are about to receive some knocks to their ego. Their current value in the market may not be what they think it should be – in fact, it probably isn't. There will likely be a younger candidate who could do the job, fit into the corporate age profile, and who is cheaper to employ.

This is hard to accept, but our experience is that you're likely to earn something in the order of 30–40 per cent *less* than you were getting. Those in their early 40s may not see such a drastic reduction, but for the over-50s it's very common that a smaller salary will be on offer. As a self-employed person you could earn *more* than you did previously, but you can also see a reduction in pay if you choose to go out on your own. (We discuss the risks of self-employment in Section Five.) Overall, we've seen that older workers usually need to reduce their salary expectations.

BIG COMPANIES VERSUS SMALL ONES

If you're still in your 40s, you may succeed in getting re-employed with a large company: a multinational or a big brand. Those over 50 have their chances vastly reduced. The corporate recruitment policies of big companies are much more regimented and hierarchy-conscious than small firms. And as we said above, the people doing the hiring are younger than you. They've adopted the policy and they're ageist.

Our suggestion: if you want to get back into the mainstream (meaning a full-time job, rather than other options) seek employment with an SME (a small or medium-sized enterprise). In the UK, that's a company with 250 or fewer employees. You'll have a better chance of success because the recruiter may be an older person (the MD in some cases) and your range of skills and experience will be more welcome. It's a general statement, but one that is supported by anecdotal evidence.

SMEs account for 99.9 per cent of all enterprises, 59.4 per cent of private sector employment and 50.1 per cent of private sector turnover[6]. Do some research in your sector to find SMEs that are growing; there may be a place for you in one of them. They come in all shapes and sizes. Professor Stephen McNair, Director of the Centre for Research into the Older Workforce (CROW) says that approximately one-third of UK SMEs are actually 'lifestyle businesses' (see Chapter 14) that don't require extra staff, or they are 'start-ups' run by young entrepreneurs who aren't interested in hiring older workers. That leaves two-thirds of all SMEs that may require you and your skills. That's a lot of companies.

ESSENTIALS FOR SUCCESS

In addition to adopting and developing strategies to counter age stereotypes, we've seen people succeed when they have the following:

- a robust attitude because they must be able to handle rejection;
- a capacity to demonstrate passion and enthusiasm;
- the ability to sell themselves;
- a workable plan – with options, should it not succeed;
- a useful network; and
- motivation.

If you've just read the list and you're experiencing a feeling of dismay because you don't possess these attributes, don't worry. Every item listed above is discussed in some detail in this book. You can develop in each respective area over time.

Here are some general tips:

- try to find the *right* place for yourself;
- if you can't do the same thing, try something else;

- be flexible in your attitude to position and salary;
- seek advice and take advice; and
- upgrade your skills.

AGE AND EMPLOYMENT

As they say on television, 'if you don't want to know the score, look away now.' Overall, we've had two reactions to the following material: some are put off by what appears to be 'too much negative information' with regard to age and employment, while others are comforted by the knowledge that redundancy for older workers is a fairly recent cultural phenomenon, and therefore it assists them in realising that their predicament is not their fault. The information in this panel isn't essential in helping you with your work search. However, in Chapter 5 you're asked to create a personal strategy. The following content will aid you in devising a realistic plan.

As well as conducting our own research, we interviewed Dr Chris Ball, Chief Executive of The Age and Employment Network (TAEN), an independent not-for-profit organisation whose mission is to make the labour market work for people in mid- and later life. We also spoke with Professor Stephen McNair, who we introduced earlier in the chapter.

A brief history of modern redundancy

It's useful to have a historical context in order to understand why we have an ageist working culture. At the beginning of the 1970s, the usual age for men to quit employment was 67 and jobs for life still existed. After World War II, worldwide recessions had yet to become a regular occurrence. The recession of the 1970s was triggered by an oil crisis. Britain saw a three-day week and a massive hike in the numbers of older workers losing their jobs. Many of them – even highly trained professionals – remained out of work. Labour unrest was a problem and one that got bigger in

1979, when Margaret Thatcher was elected. She introduced monetarist polices, eliminated inefficient industries, and the result was a recession, with unemployment figures doubling from 1.5 million to more than 3 million. This coincided with a global recession in 1983. Again, older workers bore the brunt of the lay-offs. As a business strategy, companies made older workers redundant first, in order to control costs. The trend continues today.

Concurrent with these recessions, Britain was developing a pension scheme that was the envy of the world, but only for certain sectors: large corporations and some parts of the public sector. The Redundancy Payments Act (1965) ensured some compensation to those who were laid off; compensation that would increase and become part of what we know as 'the package'. There was a desire to avoid unrest when redundancies were necessary, so packages were made larger and people left willingly. They volunteered to go because it was advantageous. Some were able to add to their package by drawing on a pension after the age of 50, with the pension fund bearing the cost.

The 1980s saw the creation of a culture of compensation. People wanted the package. Voluntary redundancies (VR) and early retirement (ER) became commonplace. Many people took ER, with a generous nest egg, and some were able to retire comfortably at age 52, set up for life.

This lasted through the 1990s, but it was a historical anomaly that took place over a brief period of time, roughly two decades, ending around the year 2000 (for most sectors). It was illusory to believe that the compensation culture could be maintained indefinitely. It doesn't make economic sense to pay people *not to work*; it's akin to the agricultural policy where farmers were paid *not to grow* certain crops that were in surplus. In the long term, both policies were unsustainable.

Demographic change

In 2011, the first baby boomers reached age 65, the State Pension Age for men (which is now being modified and moved upwards[7]). The exact dates of the end of the postwar baby boom are disputed – they vary from country to country – but the size of the population group that it describes is not in doubt. This is the 'silver tsunami', the demographic wave that is breaking on the shores of Western nations.

It has also been called a 'demographic time bomb', one that companies have known about for decades. They've talked about it as if it was a terrible thing. And yet they did nothing to address the issue – they didn't even build a breakwater against the wave. Instead, they thought they could maintain young, thrusting organisations, and do this by avoiding retention of older workers. According to Dr Chris Ball:

> 'They dealt with fluctuating labour needs by a combination of misguided approaches, most significantly declaring people redundant whenever the barometer pointed to "change". They took the opportunity (as they saw it) to cut back the "dead wood" in their organisations, and since dead wood typically comprised older workers they made a virtue of youthfulness, seeing their energy but often ignoring the callowness that youth occasionally presents. The era of the over-promoted young executive dawned, in which youth was the answer to everything and age was seen as having little to offer. At the precise time that we should have been realising that demographic change was issuing a new challenge to keep working rather longer, employers began cutting people off at the knees in their early fifties.'[8]

Companies stopped developing older employees; they failed to make them versatile. Many were left in the same jobs without professional development, waiting for an inevitable redundancy.

In her book, *Career Crunch!*, Helen Hallpike expresses it another way:

> 'Major demographic movements have created a youth culture and, although this will be a passing phenomenon, ruthless corporate streamlining has used it to reshape our present career patterns.'[9]

The bomb explodes

Our society is ageing. People are living longer than they used to, and they're having fewer children. That means the number of young people is shrinking, with a consequent reduction in those who have valuable skills[10].

Dr Chris Ball says:

> 'If there was a demographic time bomb, then that time bomb has certainly stopped ticking. Indeed, as the first of the baby boomers have retired, taking their skills and knowledge with them, you could say that the time bomb has gone off. More of a cluster bomb, however – this is no massive explosion but a rippling firecracker of damage that will reverberate through the next decades of the century.'

By the early 2020s, one in three workers in the UK will be over 50[11]. The impact on employment cannot be ignored. 'All the projections that we have indicate that there will be a chronic shortage of labour over the next ten years,' says Professor McNair[12]. He cites the UK Commission on Employment and Skills (UKCES) 'Working Futures 2004–2014 Sectoral Report', which indicates that by 2017, 12 million people will have left the workforce, with only 7 million entering. That will mean a net requirement of 5 million workers. McNair says the replacement demand for jobs will be eight times greater than the number of new jobs. At the same time, governments are struggling to cope with underfunded pension schemes. People will have to work longer; older workers can't be sidelined. Ball says that demographic pressure alone will not make change happen, we can't rely on anti-discrimination legislation and age diversification policies. They are essential, but insufficient to address the issues of an ageing population. Instead, companies must have a valid business case for retaining older workers. Professor McNair states that it is unfair to say that all employers are not changing their ways. He's seen evidence that some of them are, including some multinationals. But in his words, 'most employers don't look very far ahead.'

And so they need you out there but they don't know it yet. For people currently in their 40s, the future is bright. There is every possibility that, out of sheer necessity, hiring practices will change over the next ten years so that older workers are retained. However, those in their 50s face more of a struggle in the next decade. We predict that companies will have adopted less ageist policies by 2020, but it's not possible to know the rate of change. It could be within five years, it may take longer. One thing is certain: ageism will diminish over time. According to McNair, 'People's attitudes may not change, but their behaviour will have to.'

SUMMARY

You've met the 'seven elephants in the room' and learned how to deal with them. We've offered some advice on managing your salary expectations and on the size of companies that might welcome older workers, with general tips to aid you on your way. If you've read the panel on age and employment, you know how our ageist working culture was developed, and you've heard from two experts who have offered their opinions on what the future may bring. You can apply that knowledge later, in your 'winning strategy' that you will develop in Chapter 5.

Finally, we think it's a good idea to heed Dr Ball's advice: 'You can't afford to rest on your laurels. People today have to be relentlessly determined to upgrade their competency and skills.' And we agree with Professor McNair: things are changing and there is reason for optimism. In the long term, age barriers to employment are going to come down. The ageing workforce is too large and important to ignore. Age discrimination may not be defeated any time soon, but it can be overcome by cleverness and persistence. Those of us who are older have talent and wisdom; we are valuable in society, and we are crafty enough to develop new strategies for success. Our services are required.

SUCCESS STORY: JOHN MCGEE

It's very unusual for an older worker to find a job after only four months of unemployment, especially if the redundancy occurred during a recession and that worker is over 60. John McGee was able to get a new job because of his confidence in self-presentation during the interview, when he boldly addressed the elephant in the room: his age.

His early education was varied, and it did not include any time at university – that came later. Nonetheless, he developed a good career in facilities management, working in the IT sector. From 1982–84 he was Property Project Manager for Wang, moving on to become Facilities Manager for Prime and then Morgan Stanley. This was followed by a ten-year stint as UK Facilities Manager at Tandem, which ended shortly after their merger with Compaq in 1997. John was offered a generous redundancy package in 1998, and he was only out of work for three weeks (at age 51). It's worth noting that all of his jobs were gained through networking, including his next position at ICO, a satellite communications company, where he was Head of Real Estate and Facilities from 1998–2001. That job came about because the HR Director at ICO came from Tandem. When ICO were forced to reduce their headcount dramatically in 2001 (his second redundancy) John stayed on for a year as a consultant, helping to sell properties and move staff. He had another year as a freelance, working for a health and safety company, where a former supplier became a client.

John's health and safety qualifications are essential to the next part of the story. He acquired a NEBOSH diploma in 1999, and then, in 2003, a Masters Degree in Health and Safety Law and Environmental Law (with distinction) from the University of Salford. In 2004, after two years as a consultant, he decided that the freelance life was not for him and he got a position as Health and Safety Manager with the chartered surveyors, Lee Baron. After four years, he sensed a redundancy looming, which he pre-empted by working his network of contacts and finding another job. With the recession taking hold, this job lasted only six months, ending in December 2008.

In four months of unemployment John had ten interviews and he says the biggest obstacle he has had to overcome was his age. He's certain that, had he been younger, he would have been taken more seriously. When he saw an advertisement for a position as Health and Safety Manager with MOAT, he applied, knowing that it would mean switching sectors from private to public (social housing). He had no contacts or experience in the sector, but in the interview he sold himself as a man with experience, someone with gravitas – important attributes for a person in a health and safety position. John has a background in amateur theatre and he's convinced that, as well as finding the right employer, his self-presentation skills got him the job.

John is working for a company that values age. Although he's earning less than he was ten years ago, he enjoys his job and likes the fact that he's making a positive contribution to society. His advice: be determined, present your age as an advantage, and hone your presentation skills.

COPING WITH REDUNDANCY

2

THE ROLE, NOT THE PERSON

It's the question most asked at parties: 'And what do you do?' Until now, you've had a ready answer and, even if you didn't like your job, your place in the world was established – both for yourself and for the questioner. If you are unemployed, your response to the question is likely to be something along the lines of: 'I've recently been made redundant', or 'I'm looking for work'. We suggest you give another response, one that is framed in positive terms and is actually a more truthful comment: 'My role was made redundant. I'm looking at new opportunities.' This is a better way of describing yourself: not as an unfortunate person, but as someone who has been given a new opportunity. If your redundancy was involuntary, it may not feel this way at first; being let go is a dreadful experience, no matter how it occurs. But it might help to consider something else: you are not responsible for the business structures in which we operate. Unless you've been grossly incompetent or you've embezzled money, it's unlikely that your redundancy has been entirely your fault. Your *role* was made redundant, not *you* as a person.

If your redundancy was voluntary, and you are happy about it, this chapter may not seem relevant. However, should your time of unemployment extend beyond what you have planned, you may find some benefit in what follows.

EMOTIONAL ISSUES

In spite of the above, even knowing you are blameless, it is impossible not to take redundancy personally. For most of us, our work is the thing that defines who we are, and taking it away reduces us in stature. So it's important to remember that you are more than a job description: you have talent, intelligence, experience, a network of friends and family, and you can use these things to find new work, whether it's a job or a form of self-employment. As a mature person, you possess a wide range of useful skills. Framing redundancy as an opportunity will allow you to build on your experience and recreate a successful working life. It's waiting for you, once you get over a period of grieving.

THE FIVE STAGES OF LOSS

Elisabeth Kübler-Ross, a Swiss-born psychiatrist, proposed the theory that people who know they are dying will experience five stages of grief; so do those who have lost a loved one. This concept was developed further in her work with David Kessler, and the stages were renamed 'the five stages of loss'[1]. Since work is such an important part of identity, losing it always has serious emotional repercussions, and so we use the theory here to explain the emotional reactions that workers commonly have when a redundancy occurs.

The stages described by Kübler-Ross are: denial, anger, bargaining, depression, and acceptance. They are experienced by most people but not necessarily in that order. The length of time spent in each stage will vary according to the individual. Sometimes a person can experience all of the stages in the same day.

1. Denial

'*This can't be happening to me*', or perhaps, '*I can't believe this little upstart is giving me the sack*', may have been among the thoughts in your mind the day you sat in the HR office, or received your letter of notice.

Denial will always involve blame. You will probably blame yourself or your colleagues, the company, the economy, the greedy bankers that got us into this mess – and you may be right, but your situation remains the same.

2. Anger

When blame is attached, anger is close behind. Most of us have an innate sense of justice; losing your job will transgress your own rules of fairness. If you don't deserve this, then it is worth getting angry about. Who are they to take your livelihood away, and in such a callous fashion? This, of course, is why people are given a box, ten minutes to pack under supervision, and then are escorted out of the building by a security guard. You may still be angry over what happened to you, but you will get over it.

3. Bargaining

'Isn't there some other way of handling this problem?'; *'Can I stay if I take reduced hours?'*; *'Are you sure that I'm the right person to be let go?'*; *'Shouldn't you be looking at someone else?'* Any manager or professional knows how to make a deal, and there was never a better time than when you sat in that office. You probably tried bargaining or, if you were not given the opportunity, you've wondered if you can negotiate your way back into the company. But there are times when no amount of bargaining is going to work; sometimes you cannot make a deal.

4. Depression

After you've lost this important part of your life, and you know you can't get it back – that's when depression arrives. It sounds dramatic, but this is the most dangerous stage of all, one that leads some people to suicide. We've all heard stories of people so desperate that they have chosen this option because they cannot envisage a future worth living, and their current state is unbearable. The power of the mind to alter body chemistry is well known, so be on guard against unrealistic thoughts that drag you down in a spiral of negativity. Some of the symptoms of clinical depression are: constant anxiety; sleeplessness; loss of appetite; blaming yourself entirely for your situation; a general feeling of numbness; and continuously thinking that nothing will improve in your life.

If you find yourself seriously thinking suicidal thoughts, seek help immediately. Put this book down and resolve your situation before proceeding.

5. Acceptance

This is a goal, a destination that you reach after making a difficult journey. You'll know you've arrived when you realise that you haven't been upset for a few days or weeks, and you can think clearly about your situation. Having passed through the first four stages, you're now ready to move on.

How we experience these stages, the order and the amount of time involved, varies with each individual. Some people bounce back in a few weeks, while others may take months or years. Comparisons with your own predicament are useless, because whoever you compare yourself with isn't you. Give yourself time, and consider what Kübler-Ross said in an interview:

> 'In Switzerland I was educated in line with the basic premise: work, work, work. You are only a valuable human being if you work. This is utterly wrong. Half working, half dancing – that is the right mixture. I myself have danced and played too little.'[2]

SHAME

This is not a stage of loss, but it is an emotion that must be reckoned with when you are made redundant. Since we have a working culture that defines people in terms of productivity and earnings, those who are not gainfully employed are sometimes ostracised socially – shunned even, in some cases. They belong in a different category: the unskilled, the spongers. Questions arise: *Isn't it likely that someone who has been made redundant at mid or senior level is incompetent?* or *Don't people get what they deserve?*

'The best rise to the top; the worst sink to the bottom' is a saying that most of us are familiar with, and even though we may believe in a philosophy of tolerance and understanding – looking out for the little guy – in reality the working world is cruel. Judgements fall hard and fast, and we know we will be judged by others because we have done it ourselves. Now is the time to have a look at how this type of thinking will affect your ability to move forward.

There are two kinds of shame: healthy and unhealthy. Healthy shame comes in the form of embarrassment about something we have done that is in our control. Being naked in a public place, taking something that doesn't belong to us, blurting out thoughtless and awkward words in a social situation, these are examples of the causes of healthy shame. It's something that encourages social cohesion, with norms that are defined by the society in which we live. When someone breaks these rules we call them 'shameless'.

Unhealthy shame is a sense that something is basically wrong with us; we are somehow flawed as persons. This is the one to watch out for. Most often, unhealthy shame comes out of our own upbringing. Those who have been raised by critical, overbearing parents will have been given a strong dose of unhealthy shame. Age can contribute to shame because there are plenty of older, successful people with whom you can compare yourself. Your friends or family members could be doing well, the neighbours might still be flaunting their wealth, and here you are, seeking work at your age. You might feel ashamed about it.

If you do, you are not alone. Lots of mature people – including the very competent – have been made redundant. It's important to remember that everyone has to deal with strong emotions, especially at the beginning of a time of unemployment. These feelings will pass and the time it takes will vary with each individual.

HELP IS AT HAND

You will need some responses for questions that are lurking in the background, such as: *What will a prospective employer think?* After all, if the company didn't go bust, and only some people were made redundant, why did they pick you? It's important to have some answers ready, and to settle these questions in your own mind.

This book will show you how to prepare and deliver a TMAY: **T**ell **M**e **A**bout **Y**ourself (also known as an elevator pitch). It's a brief description of you that exudes confidence (see Chapter 7). You'll also learn how to work out the best way for you to respond to difficult questions.

FINANCIAL ISSUES

It's essential to prepare a budget for the coming months, detailing your expenses against the resources at hand. A simple spreadsheet will do the job. For most people, the big worries are keeping the house and maintaining payments on loans and credit cards. For those with school-age children, the cost of their education must also be considered. Hard choices will likely have to be made, and now is the time to consider what economies can be achieved. What can you live without?

Your budget should point the way to making a financial plan that is sustainable over the course of a year or more. That may seem like a long time, and you may be re-employed sooner, but it's best to take a longer view. We recommend economising immediately, as a safety measure should re-employment take longer than you imagine.

SIGNING ON

At first, many professionals will not consider taking this course of action, because it seems unnecessary – £65 a week on Jobseeker's Allowance isn't very much, so why bother? But if you think of it as a means to economise, then signing on may have a different appearance. You could be entitled to a range of other benefits: your National Insurance will continue to be paid; you may qualify for a reduction in Council Tax; and after 13 weeks you can receive support for mortgage interest. There could be free access or reduced rates for certain local facilities and other things like dental care, prescriptions, eye tests, partially-subsidised eyeglasses, and discounted travel.

In terms of job search, the government has recently made some efforts to provide help for professionals and managers. The problem seems to be that, at local office level, staff at Jobcentre Plus are often not aware of what is available, so you may need to tell them what programme is applicable to you. 'Careerplan4.me' is a web-based service for executives, and another new programme is 'Job Search Support for Newly Unemployed Professionals', which is a one-day package of focused support (at the time of writing). Persistence may be required, so we suggest that you arrive at the Jobcentre with information and website addresses that you have researched beforehand. Be prepared to tell them what it is you have in mind.

In all cases, none of the benefits or programmes described above can be accessed without signing on. Google 'Jobcentre Plus' and you'll find a list of websites that you can visit to help you determine your entitlement, and the location of your local office. Book an appointment, make a list of questions that you want to ask, and arrive on time with your required documentation. Walking into a Jobcentre may feel strange because they weren't designed for executives in need of work. You will be called a 'customer' by the staff, and you will likely be treated with courtesy and respect, but explaining your circumstances to a total stranger in an open-plan office is uncomfortable.

Think of this as a temporary measure – an aid to your budget – and the experience will be less difficult. Remember that you've been paying for this service with your taxes for many years. You are entitled to it.

COPING STRATEGIES

Even if your redundancy was voluntary, you have lost control of a large part of your life. It's important to get back a sense of being in charge, and to develop a positive attitude to your predicament. Some practical ways of doing this are outlined below.

Exercise

It's true that exercise makes us feel better. We're not suggesting joining a gym and working your stress out on a machine or a set of weights – although if that is your regular practice, by all means stay with it. Exercise need not be complicated or expensive: a daily walk will do the trick. Just 30 minutes of brisk walking is enough to raise your heart rate to a beneficial level; endorphins will kick in and result in a feeling of well-being. The important thing is doing something regularly and making sure that you get out of the house. Not only will you feel better physically, but sticking with a simple discipline will help you establish a routine.

Job clubs

The benefits are enormous: a place to go once a week where you can learn to improve your presentation skills and be with people who understand what you're going through. A good job club will be a combination of back-to-work course, social club, and networking opportunity. It's also a place to practise your TMAY in a friendly environment. You will need feedback on your self-presentation skills; it's essential that they be honed and refined.

This type of club is one of the best you could join, even if it means travelling some distance or having to pay. Free clubs for older, white-collar workers are thin on the ground. Until 2009, they were all in Berkshire, but that situation has changed. Free and fee-paying clubs are springing up around the country. You can find a listing of active clubs on **www.gbjobclubs.org** (click 'Job Club Directory' on the homepage). Not all of them will be suitable for older workers, so try to have a word with someone at the club beforehand to determine if it's right for you.

Personal support groups

Most of your friends will still be employed and their lives and routines will continue as before. It's you that has changed. You may feel strange around your working friends, uncertain as to whether or not they are judging you. Even good friends may not be supportive, especially if they've never had personal experience of redundancy. If a job club is not possible, consider forming a network of supportive people. Begin with one person. It needn't be a friend; a former colleague or a neighbour will do for a start. Meet weekly at a regular time and at a location away from your respective homes. That way you'll be going out again. Discuss job and career possibilities, swap information, and agree to be supportive and telephone each other at difficult times. You can build your group over time. The important thing is that you are with people who understand your experience; they will help you, and you will help them.

Women are likely to find this suggestion amenable. Men tend to isolate themselves because admitting weakness is unmanly and frowned upon. But remember that your former workplace was a support group; your colleagues who shared your experience upported you as part of a team.

The key thing is to avoid isolation. Spending all day at your computer will not result in a job or get you new clients if you decide to be self-employed. Positive social interaction will boost your confidence and increase your chances of success.

Career consultants

You may consider paying a career management company, or an individual career consultant, to help you assess and define your skills and prepare for re-entry into the job market. It will not provide the social interaction of a job club, but you'll receive a higher level of direct support. There won't be a guarantee that you will be re-employed, but your chances can be greatly improved.

Volunteering

This is one of the best ways to improve self-esteem and help maintain a positive attitude. It has been said that, as long as you're helping someone else, you don't have a problem. If there is an organisation that you've always meant to support, now is the time. As well as getting you out of the house, volunteering will expand your social network, something that may pay off with a job offer.

Hobbies

Most have us have meant to do something that our work lives have prevented. If you've wanted to study another language, learn a musical instrument, take up golf or become a better tennis player, do it now. A lot of people develop a second career out of their special interests or hobbies. This need not be your objective, as learning or developing any skill is its own reward.

SUMMARY

Remember that your *role* was made redundant, not *you* as a person. You are much more than a job description. Realise that it takes time to get over what is a very difficult and emotionally trying experience. Make a financial plan for yourself and sign on if necessary. Avoid isolation, and try to incorporate the following coping mechanisms into your routine:

- exercise;
- join a job club;
- form a support group;
- volunteer; and
- develop a special interest or hobby.

Be sure to start your search for work as soon as possible.

LOOKING AHEAD

You will need to take stock of your situation and determine an effective course of action. Sending out applications for any opportunities that look vaguely promising is a normal reaction, but one that should be resisted. New members often arrive at their first job club meeting and talk about the numbers of CVs they've sent, matched against responses, and then arriving at a hypothetical number of interviews that should have resulted from this type of approach. They wonder why they haven't hit their target for interviews. It's because this mathematical procedure – if you apply for enough jobs, sooner or later you'll get one – may have worked when you were younger, but it won't work now. It feels good because you are *doing* something, at a time when constructive activity is a requirement for maintaining emotional balance. It is laudable, but not very practical.

This isn't a numbers game. It's not the volume of applications sent, it's *what* you apply for and *how* you apply that matter. You may decide that self-employment is the solution to your predicament. By working through the exercises and following the recommendations in this book, your chances of success will be vastly increased. So have faith, be patient, and press on.

SUCCESS STORY: **TREVOR GENT**

Trevor's first redundancy occurred when he was 41. He was re-employed within a week. Therefore, he was certain it would be easy to get another job when he took a voluntary redundancy at age 49. Trevor could not have been more wrong. No one queued up to hire him, and he was devastated to learn that he was not immediately perceived as the desirable employee he thought he was. He soon wished he had found a new role before taking redundancy, because it took him two-and-a-half years to find a new job. On his journey to re-employment he encountered many obstacles that an older worker must face. He persevered and succeeded in finding a job that makes him look forward to getting up in the morning and going to work.

A qualified telecoms engineer, Trevor graduated from the University of Sheffield in 1980. After working for nine years at GEC Telecoms, he spent seven years at Nortel, working at the Maidenhead lab of Bell Northern Research, anglicising their North American products. In 1996, he made a sector change from telecoms to cable TV and, after a few jobs, he subsequently worked for nine years at NTL (it was called Cable Tel when he joined) first as Regional Director, then Head of Engineering, Director of Acquisitions Support and, finally, Director of Voice Engineering. He left the company in 2006 when a merger with Telewest meant a change in corporate culture. Trevor chose redundancy. As it turned out, Virgin soon became the only cable company in the UK, limiting Trevor's future chances in the sector.

He decided first to look for jobs in telecoms because there weren't suitable options in cable. It was then that he met his first obstacle: the industry had changed drastically, he had no mobile or IP experience, and he was unknown as a person who had changed technology sectors at director level. His second hurdle was more personal: it took him one-and-a-half years to discover that nothing captured his interest. Trevor only applied for jobs because he thought he should, not because he wanted what was on offer. Therefore, he was uninspiring as a prospect. He says the key to his re-employment was getting to know himself. He worked with a careers counsellor to identify what he actually found interesting and exciting. For Trevor, it was helping people combined with a technical challenge.

Armed with this knowledge, he was able to act on an opportunity that he might have previously overlooked: applying for a position as Principal Telecoms Engineer with Crossrail. A former boss thought he could do the job, and so his CV was passed to his future employer, an informal chat took place, and Trevor was able to sell his skills with confidence and enthusiasm. He carried that attitude forward through the formal interview and selection process, ultimately winning the job.

He's been told that his experience outside the railway sector makes him valuable at Crossrail. He likes the fact that his work affects people in their everyday lives, and his main challenge is to find a migration path to update out-of-date equipment. So his job fulfils his two main interests: helping people plus a technical challenge.

Trevor's advice for older jobseekers:

- get to know yourself;
- whatever you apply for, apply with passion;
- know you're the best person for the job.

There are a few things in Trevor's story that will be reiterated in this book. First: identify your skills and interests. Understanding who you are and what motivates you will enable you to sell yourself in any situation. Second: networking is essential. Trevor found his job through his network; a former boss recommended him. Third: be prepared take your transferable skills and experience and apply them to another sector. Trevor would not otherwise have considered the rail sector. Fourth: be prepared to take a lower salary. Trevor is earning 40 per cent less than he did in his previous job, but he's not suffering financially, as he was previously on £100,000 annually. And he doesn't mind because, at age 52, he's a man who loves his work.

SECTION

2

Motivation, Assessment, Strategy and Action

MOTIVATE YOURSELF 3

At a seminar on 'Motivation for Jobseekers', a fellow delegate confessed he wasn't that impressed. He was expecting to hear a motivational speech, rather than a talk about motivation. When asked what he remembered from a previous motivational speech, he said: 'Oh, nothing much, but I felt really good afterwards.'

You can watch the world's top motivational speakers on YouTube or attend one of their events. Hearing a motivational speech might have a feel-good factor, but it doesn't teach you how to motivate yourself on a Monday morning after yet another rejection e-mail, failed interview or lost opportunity. You know that you *should* do more networking or pick up the phone to speak to the head-hunter as promised, but you just can't get motivated.

This chapter is not a motivational speech. The aim is to help you understand what motivates *you* and, having understood that, to practise self-motivation on an ongoing basis. The motivated jobseeker has clearly defined goals. He or she devotes an appropriate amount of time each day to job-hunting activities and uses the time between jobs effectively, by engaging in a range of activities: consulting, working part-time, retraining or volunteering.

The unmotivated jobseeker is different. He or she applies for jobs sporadically and without a specific objective, has difficulty setting targets and finds the overall goal of re-employment increasingly daunting. Days and weeks seem to merge into one.

You may experience a mixture of both. The challenge is to turn the unmotivated days into productive time. In order to accomplish this it helps to understand what 'motivation' means to you, so you can learn how to motivate yourself. It will serve you well, not only when job-seeking but also in your future career.

UNDERSTANDING MOTIVATION

A dictionary definition of 'motivate' is 'to cause to act in a particular way' or 'to stimulate interest in a person doing a task'[1]. For our purposes we prefer a description that links to a level of self-confidence. A motivated jobseeker is one who is clear about what actions he or she should take in order to find a job, and has the energy and confidence to take the right action at the right time.

Many at the Job Club report that they know what they *should* be doing, but don't feel motivated enough to take action. Often this apathy relates to a past experience. 'I really can't face the thought of working for a boss like that again,' they say, or 'All that hard work just to end up being made redundant'. Lack of motivation can also be due to the way someone thinks about the future. 'Why should I work just to make someone else rich?' is a demotivating thought about an event that hasn't happened yet. Sometimes people are uninspired because what they think they should do is based on someone else's recommendation, and so there is no personal enthusiasm for the task and, therefore, no real desire to make it happen.

If the fire of enthusiasm that drove you from job to job in your earlier career has gone out, or is reduced to barely glowing embers, how do you rekindle it? The answer is by dealing with the past, getting inspired to take action and continuing to stay motivated.

1. DEAL WITH THE PAST – WHY ARE YOU HERE NOW?

A common cause of low motivation is bitterness or unhappiness about work situations that have led to a person's current status. It's impossible to plan and take positive action for the future because the sense of being wronged is so powerful that it colours every action. Often there is a sense of injustice or cynicism about being made redundant: 'It was a typical bad decision, no more than I'd come to expect of the management of that company', someone might say. Or they could be thinking, *I wasn't competent enough,* or *I'm no good at company politics,* or maybe *I'm just getting too old and slow and out of touch with technology.*

Being motivated is a state of mind where we reflect on lessons learned from the past rather than wishing we'd done things differently.

In the here and now, we are committed to taking the actions we need to take, with a clear and inspiring outcome in mind.

The first step in dealing with the past is to look at it rationally and objectively. In the previous chapter, we discussed how the feelings of grief at being let go from a job are a normal part of the way we deal with redundancy. It's easy to further interpret the event as a slight on your personal ability, or to question the validity of the management decision. However, it is now common for redundancy to appear on a CV at least once. Some business reasons for a redundancy are:

- market forces result in downsizing;
- competition in the sector forces a strategic change;
- economic downturn leads to all companies losing staff;
- budget cuts mean that 20 per cent of staff have to be released;
- skills no longer needed or relevant after a change in business strategy;
- new management wants to bring in their own support team;
- company reorganisation makes department heads unnecessary;
- company merger or acquisition eliminates duplicate roles.

It's important to talk about your current situation in terms of the external situations that led to it. Being able to discuss the business factors that led to your redundancy disassociates the situation from yourself and your own reputation. Highly skilled, experienced and well-networked people get made redundant when corporate strategy dictates that their specialism is no longer required. To assume that your redundancy is a reflection on your capabilities is to turn an external reason into an internal one, which diminishes self-confidence and reduces motivation. It is critical to know which reasons are external in order to be able to rationally explain it to yourself. Later, you will use the same narrative with potential employers and clients. Stop blaming yourself. Consider mistakes and errors as useful lessons learned and take action if required, without seeking to apportion blame.

You must, however, acknowledge any aspects of your performance or behaviour that may have contributed to your redundancy. These are internal reasons. You owe it to yourself to check with a partner, friend or coach, or anyone who will be objective. You might identify some areas of weakness that you can do something about. They may have been specific to your situation. If you were not suited to the role, it's appropriate to admit it and seek out a job that matches your skills and capabilities. Remaining in an unsuitable position would naturally have resulted in lower performance, negative feedback and the resulting blow to your confidence and motivation. Any weakness will be exacerbated by a stressful environment. On the other hand, if you were in a work culture that suited your strengths, those perceived weaknesses may have been unnoticed by anyone apart from you, so you may not see any benefit in addressing them.

The key point about any personal weaknesses is to act on those that are important in getting the next role. You don't have to fix everything. Acknowledge that some of them are just a feature of the way you are, and manage them accordingly. As an example, consider someone who quits four successive jobs because of a difference of opinion with his boss, and who has excused his behaviour by saying he doesn't feel valued. To move on, he may need to acknowledge he has an aversion to working for a boss within an organisation. He might want to consider becoming self-employed.

2. GET INSPIRED TO TAKE ACTION

No reference to motivation would be complete without a reflection on the work of Abraham Maslow. In his book *Motivation and Personality*[2], he describes what is now known widely as 'Maslow's Hierarchy of Needs'. In Figure. 3.1 we have adapted his concept for those seeking work.

In essence, Maslow stated that humans will satisfy their needs in order of priority. Clearly the need for food, air and water is a higher priority than the need for being part of a social community, which in turn is normally a higher priority than long-term career satisfaction. However, when one level of needs is met, then the next level up becomes a priority, hence the hierarchy.

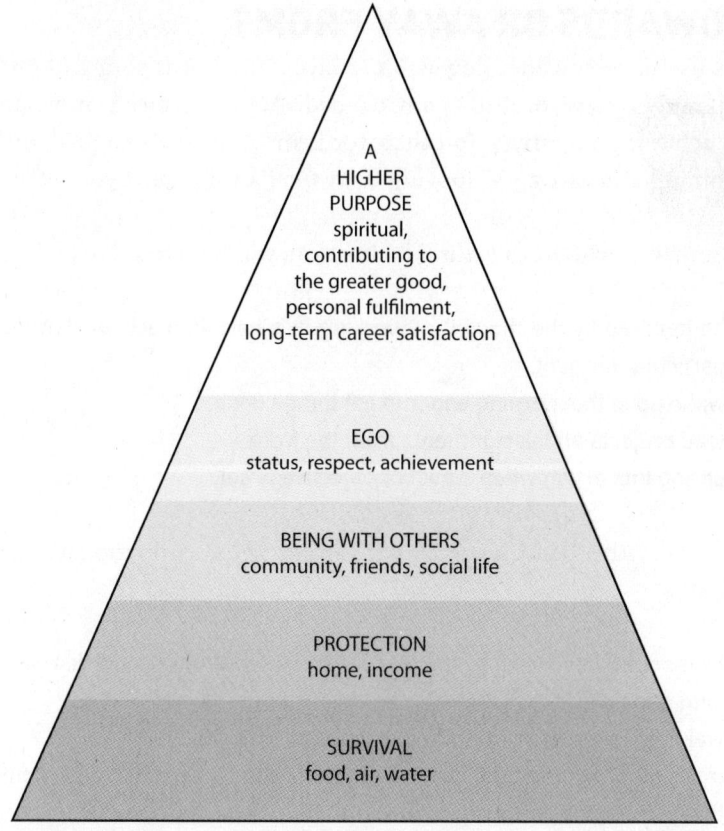

Fig 3.1 Hierarchy of Work and Career Needs (based on Maslow's Hierarchy of Needs)

Consider the case of a male executive who has been made redundant, or who has taken early retirement. He's achieved his dream of a well-appointed detached house in the country and he's paid off the mortgage. If his prime motivation for working throughout his career had been providing a secure, idyllic home for himself and his dependants, he might, perhaps, unconsciously feel that his motivating need has now been met. Why work again? Eventually, his higher need for ego and status begins to suffer as he is no longer contributing actively to society. He feels the need to earn respect. At this point, his motivation returns and he commits himself to taking on leading roles in the community.

TOWARDS OR AWAY FROM?

It's useful to consider how you perceive a need: is it something you aspire to achieve, or is it a pain avoided? Are you typically motivated by achieving objectives, in other words moving *towards* a goal, or by avoiding a negative, i.e. moving *away from* an outcome you want to avoid.

Someone who has a *towards* inclination, will tend to:

- be inspired by the thought of working in a certain place, or earning a particular amount;
- wake up in the morning eager to get things done;
- lead projects and assignments from the front;
- spring into action when a goal or objective is set.

On the other hand, someone with an *away from* inclination will tend to:

- be inspired into action by the fear of what their CV might look like with a long gap on it;
- wake up in the morning with a long list of things to do;
- manage projects and assignments by trying to cater for all potential things that may go wrong;
- spring into action when it appears that the goal or objective will not be achieved.

For example, a jobseeker made redundant with a handsome pay-off has an *away from* tendency and their prime motivator was getting away from financial worries. They may well find it hard to get re-employed quickly, as that pain has now gone. It's only when the worry of financial insecurity raises its ugly head – after they've spent the money – that they will be motivated to begin their search. Their *away from* motivator has returned.

A person in the same situation who has a *towards* inclination, might find it difficult to accept that they cannot walk into a new job straight away. They are driven strongly in the direction of a new role, despite their apparent financial security. Their friends or former colleagues may wonder why they are doing it if they don't need the money. The truth is, they don't see earning money as a way of avoiding the pain of financial insecurity, but as a *towards* goal in itself.

Teams or groups can show a preference too. A sales team will tend to be very *towards* inclined if they have an inspiring sales target to accomplish. The inherent risk will be that they are so focused on achieving this target that they don't anticipate problems. It's better to have a few *away from* members on the team who are motivated by solving the team's problems and challenges, and will point out the potential pitfalls. A customer service or operations team will tend to be biased *away from* as their job is to fix customer problems and issues. Likewise, it is useful to have *towards* people on the team to set strategic direction and provide leadership when there are no customer problems to manage.

Awareness of your preferences allows you to frame job search objectives in language that motivates you. Write your goals and tasks in the way that suits you: either *towards* or *away from*.

Of course no one is completely *towards* or *away from*. Each of us exhibits a combination of the two; there is no right or wrong. As far as we know, there are as many successful, satisfied *away from* inclined people as there are *towards*. What's important is to know and understand what your personal preference is, so that you can motivate yourself.

Exercise: determining your inclination

'If you don't know where you are going, any road will get you there.'[3]

One of the keys to getting and staying motivated is to be able to state your objective in terms of *towards* or *away from,* depending on what works best for you. We'll cover the topic of setting goals in more detail in Chapters 5 and 6. Below are two examples of perfectly valid statements of the same goal.

Towards: I want to secure a senior role with a leading operator in the solar energy industry because I am inspired by the idea of combining my financial management skills with my personal passion for advancing this country's adoption of renewable energy sources.

Away from: I need to secure an income for my family by June 20th, otherwise we cannot pay the mortgage. I worry about sustainability and the environmental impact of fossil fuels. I want to help prevent a new entrant in the solar energy industry from overstretching themselves with improper financial controls as they seek to grow.

In terms of the way each is written, rather than the content, which one appeals to you most? Spend five to ten minutes, ideally with a partner (business or personal) who knows you, reviewing specific occasions in the past when you know you were highly motivated. Which inclination do you favour? In the past, were you more inspired to move *towards* a goal or *away from* a situation? What is your preference now?

3. STAYING MOTIVATED

Successful jobseekers are those who, despite all the knockbacks and rejections, remain clear about what they offer and why they are of value to an employer or client. Being made redundant and looking for work won't fill your mind with positive energy. Managing your state of mind to keep motivated during the weeks and months of a job search isn't easy but there are techniques to help.

Think back to a time when you were performing at your best. Remember how you felt about yourself and about others at that time. Think of the environment or office space you were in, the people you were with, the tools you worked with. Think of what people said about you. Recall the level of energy and enthusiasm you had for the task in hand. Think about how good it felt to be operating at the peak of your abilities.

Now imagine you could approach your job search in the same frame of mind. How much more efficient would you be at finding a job? How confident would you sound on the phone with a recruitment consultant? How much better would you be at interviews?

Your state of mind can make an enormous difference to the success of your job search. The human brain has difficulty distinguishing between a situation that really happened and one that has simply been played out in your mind. At the beginning of a job-seeking day, remind yourself of how good you felt at the times when you were performing at your best. This will make a real, positive difference to your job search. When you approach a task, any task, with a positive frame of mind, the outcome is invariably better than if you approach it cautiously, anticipating failure.

There are other things you can do to reinforce a positive frame of mind, or change your state of mind.

- When you achieve something, however small, acknowledge the achievement (*I've got an interview, I made that difficult call, I found out about a great job*) and reward yourself.
- Maintain regular contact with other people in your network, whether they are friends, business contacts, or other jobseekers. Contact people who lift your mood. Don't be shy. Use them when you need a lift.
- Refer to the 'mission statement' for your job search and repeat it to yourself when you need a lift. (We'll show you how to do this in Chapter 5.)
- Look after yourself and your health. Job-seeking is a job in itself. It's important not to neglect the welfare of the main worker: you. Just as in a normal job, you have to eat well, take time to relax, and enjoy some exercise so that when the times comes to make phone calls, send CVs or attend interviews you can do it with energy and drive.

FOLLOW YOUR PLAN

To help you stay motivated, we encourage you to make a plan for your job search (see Chapter 6). When you're feeling demotivated, it takes less effort to action a task that you have predefined than to start trying to answer the question, 'What do I need to do to get a job today?' The fact that you have a plan and you can tick off tasks as they're completed will boost your motivation, because it confirms that you're making progress towards your end goal: a job or work.

DEAL WITH REJECTION

Competition for jobs is fierce and you will have to learn to cope with rejections. They can occur at any stage. It might happen when you call to enquire about a job, when you send a CV, after a first interview or, worst of all, after a final interview when you were one of a shortlist of candidates.

Rejections are a form of feedback. You can gain from reflecting on the reasons you were rejected and then act on them. Dealing with negative feedback can mean taking difficult decisions. The sooner you take them, the greater your chance of success.

After you've been through a number of application processes (identify job, prepare and send application, interview, etc.) you will begin to get an idea of how you are perceived. What are recruiters saying about your CV? Is your telephone manner effective? After interviews, what feedback are you getting? It's important to assess the response as a whole rather than latch onto individual comments, which can be negative and misleading. One person's comment on your CV may be right or wrong. However, if you've sent out 80 copies of your CV and 20 recruitment consultants have commented on the lack of evidence regarding budgetary responsibility, then it's time to act on that message: either modify your CV to indicate that you did have budgetary responsibility or apply for jobs where that isn't a requirement.

However personal it feels, it's important to remember that rejection is the result of a business decision. In the opinion of the person recruiting, you are not the ideal person for the role specified. It does NOT mean that your skills and experience are negated. They are still valid and perfectly suited to a job. It may be that however much you wanted it, the recruiter did you a favour by not selecting you as you would not have been satisfied in the role. Think of each rejection as one more positive step towards finding the right job for you. In fact, if you're not receiving any rejections, it's possible you're not applying for enough roles.

Each time you're rejected, use the following three-step process to help you move to the next stage of your job-seeking process.

1. Accept the rejection for what it is. Whether or not you agree with the reasons given, assuming you are given some, the fact is that the application process for that particular role is over. Update your records to show when this happened.
2. Review the whole application process and any feedback you received. Decide what you have learned from it: what the company or recruiter liked about you; what your weaknesses were and the areas you need to improve on. Amend your approach based on specific feedback. List what you will do differently next time. Some examples: amend your CV; turn up earlier for the interview; prepare a scripted response to a particularly difficult question.
3. Then remind yourself, by referring back to your plan: I know what sort of job I am looking for and I know what I have to offer. The rejection is one more step towards finding that role.

Finally, do something to move another job opportunity forward: make a call, send a CV, or start preparing for an interview. By doing this you are confirming to yourself that the rejection is behind you and you are on to the next step. We haven't put a timescale on this. It might be something you can do in ten minutes. If it is a particularly disappointing rejection, it might take longer to recover. By going through the steps above, you can ensure that you will carry on, having learned from the rejection.

SUMMARY

Job-seeking can be lonely work. Your chances of early success are hugely enhanced if you approach it in a positive frame of mind, clear about what you have to offer and with the confidence to accept and deal with the inevitable rejections as you go through the process. When the low points come, and they will, it helps to understand what motivation is and how you are motivated, so that you can manage your way back to a positive frame of mind.

Looking forward to the next chapter, you'll have an opportunity to assess your skills and talents – the capabilities that will get you your next job, or help you to find work if you would like to be self-employed. If you're lacking inspiration now, you'll find plenty in the pages to come.

The table below identifies some typical examples of things that will occur throughout the job-hunting process, and what to do about them

Problem	Solution
Losing confidence in your abilities.	Rewrite your CV to refresh and update your skills presentation. Seek feedback from close friends or business contacts. Volunteer your services where they will be appreciated.
Feeling 'irrelevant' – your skills are no longer needed.	Do a reality check – are there jobs being advertised that call for your skills?
Constant knockbacks and rejections.	Persevere. Every rejection is a step towards the right job. Make sure you act on feedback received.
Not getting interviews after making frequent job applications.	Review your plan and approach. Are you under or overqualified for the job you are seeking? Get independent feedback on your CV and your job-seeking strategy.
Feeling overwhelmed, burned out.	Recharge your batteries by taking some time out from your job search. Do something you enjoy. Seek advice and support from other jobseekers.
Missing daily contact with other workers.	Seek opportunities to network with other jobseekers. Attend business networking events and seminars relevant to your industry.
Low self esteem.	Remind yourself of your capabilities and achievements. Work through the exercises in this chapter and do the self-assessment in Chapter 4. You may wish to seek external help if the problem persists.
Blaming yourself for rejection or redundancy.	Review the facts of the situation with a friend, partner or coach, and describe your situation in terms of external factors rather than assuming it's all your fault.
Having no structure to the day.	Use a daily planner and structure your days to include specific time slots for your job search tasks. Remember to diarise down-time for yourself.
Not seeing any rewards for the hard work you put into your job search.	Give yourself rewards when you complete tasks in your plan. Remember that success in your job search can be dependent on factors outside your control.
No targets to meet.	Set up a plan for your job search and define your own targets: number of calls to make per day, applications to send per week, etc. (see Chapter 6).

Table 3.1

SUCCESS STORY: **MIKE CARR**

For many older managers, a big fear is that they might have to take a job stacking shelves at Sainsbury's, Asda or B&Q (three employers who have age-friendly policies). Mike Carr did it out of necessity and then he found his way back into a management position. Mike is indomitable; he's motivated to have a job and he has always found a way to get one.

He's been working since 1970, when he graduated from Leeds University with a BA in Economics. Since then, he's held senior positions with blue-chip companies and he's been made redundant six times: four redundancies were voluntary; two were involuntary. His times of unemployment usually coincided with a recession, a corporate sale or a restructure – something that is typical for many people.

After early roles as Product Manager and Senior Business Planner, Mike was Direct Marketing Manager for Xerox from 1987–91, where he developed their telemarketing business. In 1991, he joined British Gas as Direct Marketing Manager. While he was there, his team won a second DMA (Direct Marketing Association) award. A restructure in 1994 gave him the opportunity to move to Scotland and work for Scottish Gas, where he helped to launch the brand. Four years later, he returned to British Gas, when he was asked to sort out their direct marketing campaigns. By this time he considered himself to be an expert troubleshooter and problem solver. Mike decided that it was time to move on. He left British Gas with plans to go into interim management (see Chapter 12).

It was 2002, Mike was 55, and he had a hard time finding work as an interim manager. It was difficult to get his first assignment, a common problem for those wanting to be an interim. Mike started job-hunting but he wasn't able to find anything suitable. He says he constantly faced one of the difficult questions most jobseekers are asked: 'Why did you leave?' After a time, Mike was desperate. That was when he swallowed his pride and took a job stacking shelves at Sainsbury's. While he was there, he read a copy of the in-house magazine and learned that Sainsbury's were starting a bank and that they were recruiting for marketing positions. He applied and got a job. It didn't last long – after 18 months the bank restructured, and Mike found himself looking for work again.

This time he spent money on using a service company for assistance in getting back to work. He says they helped him in his search and he received good support, including an assessment of his 'transferable skills' (more about these in Chapter 4) but in spite of spending eight hours per day on the phone and the computer, he got no results. Mike admits the problem was that he didn't network. After 12 months of unemployment he had to sell his house.

A friend called and offered him a job in telesales training, one that lasted only eight months. In 2007, he got some help from a recruitment agency. Once again he planned on going into interim management. He says the agency did a good job preparing him for interviews with clients but, as it turned out, he wasn't destined to become an interim. The agency found him a full-time role in an area he would never have considered previously. From 2007 until 2010, Mike was an area manager for Skills South East, identifying skills assessments and training to private firms. It was his first experience of working in 'the commercial public sector', where a publicly-funded operation sells services to private firms. Following the change of government in 2010, the contract was renewed but the decision was taken by SEEDA to integrate Business Link and Skills South East. That meant a radical downsizing, and Mike was made redundant. This time, he had 'career capital' (see Chapters 4 and 5) in his new area. He answered an advertisement and found a job within three months, working at East Berkshire College selling skills and training. He was 62 years old. Mike says, 'My age means that I'm not a threat to someone's growth.'

He's an example of a highly motivated older worker. Mike says he *must* have a job; he *has* to work. He is a *towards* person, someone who is always striving towards the goal of employment.

His tips for older workers are:

- know your transferable skills;
- be able to tell several stories about what you've done to make something a success; and
- look at areas you may not have considered previously.

CHAPTER 4

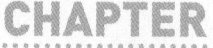

SELF-ASSESSMENT

THE WORK FUNNEL

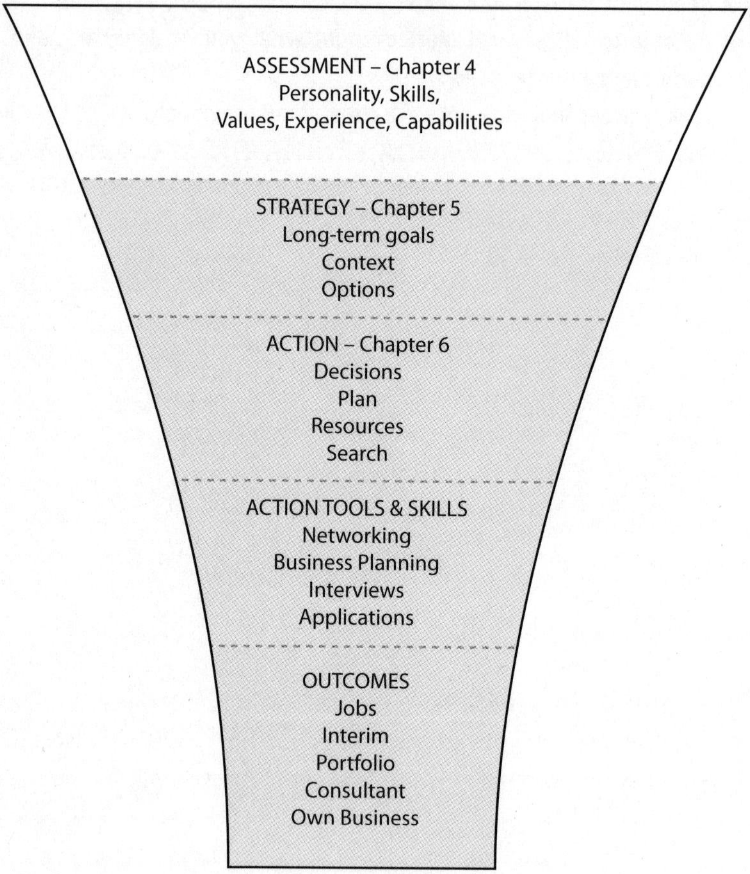
ASSESSMENT – Chapter 4
Personality, Skills,
Values, Experience, Capabilities
STRATEGY – Chapter 5
Long-term goals
Context
Options
ACTION – Chapter 6
Decisions
Plan
Resources
Search
ACTION TOOLS & SKILLS
Networking
Business Planning
Interviews
Applications
OUTCOMES
Jobs
Interim
Portfolio
Consultant
Own Business

'Know thyself', said the ancient Greeks. Now is the time to uncover more personal knowledge so you can apply it to your search for work. Whether you are reading this book after a redundancy, or you are choosing to make a job or career change, it's necessary to engage in some form of self-assessment.

Like any good business approach, it's best to start with an in-depth analysis of where you are today. Then you can make the most informed choices for the future, based on a solid foundation. Your 'career capital', the combination of experience and achievements from your life so far, allows you to position yourself for the work you want. Your values and personality traits are clues to the type of occupation and environment you should seek in order to thrive.

Complete the assessment thoroughly, before you move on to the other stages of your search for work or a job. It's important for three reasons:

1. You'll have a wealth of detail and impressive content for your CV and any verbal presentations you have to make about yourself. The level of self-awareness you will gain in this chapter will give you the confidence to be credible: you do what it says on the tin.
2. It informs you about the sorts of jobs you ought to be seeking. There are countless examples of people who have used information learned from self-assessment to make subtle but impactful changes that have enabled them to achieve greater fulfillment and success in their work.
3. Confidence is a key contributor to any successful venture, whether you're looking for a job, setting up as an interim or consultant or starting your own business. Self-assessment builds self-esteem by reminding you of your talents and past achievements. It also reveals the skills you are widely admired for having.

After completing a self-assessment you will know yourself better, be clear about what you're selling and have the confidence and credibility to get the job you want. Even if you are in work and not considering re-employment right now, self-assessment will lead to a higher degree of self-awareness that can help you in a number of ways. It can help you improve your position in your current company, decide between career options or different jobs, or decide whether self-employment is for you.

AN OVERVIEW

There are four categories of self-assessment: knowledge and experience, skills and abilities, values and aspirations, and personality. The first category includes hard facts about the industries in which you have worked, roles you have held, projects you have managed, companies or departments you have led and your qualifications and professional accreditations. These are the details that an employer will check first for signs of capability.

Skills and abilities are the underlying competencies that you bring to any role or task. There will be a huge amount of crossover between your professional and personal life. For example, a finance director may well have an excellent eye for detail and, in his spare time, put this skill to use by managing the complexity of a social enterprise. Skills can often be so intuitive that they become difficult to identify and describe. We may speak in general terms about someone having financial expertise, but we don't acknowledge that this might rely on an underlying skill of having an eye for detail. When changing career or companies, it's often far more useful to describe your underlying or core skills than the specific areas you have worked in, so that an employer or recruiter can see how your skills are transferable.

Values and aspirations are important to factor into your self-assessment because they impact directly on job satisfaction in the long term. Businesses espouse the values they hold but we often don't refer to ourselves in terms of values. Your values are the principles and standards that you hold to be true about yourself or your situation.

- I am an *honest* person.
- I value *integrity* in all my staff.
- I am a very *loyal* employee.
- I believe in *money* as the secret of success.
- Life should be *fair*.

Understanding your values is also the key to being able to judge whether an office culture or type of work is right for you. For example, if you hold strong values around non-violence, harmony and being nice to people, you may not be cut out for a role with an arms trading company.

Your personality traits will have a bearing on the sort of work that suits you best. As a manager or professional, you are almost certain to have undertaken some personality or psychometric tests during your employment. These will have provided you with an indication of the personality traits you display when interacting with other people and when you're working on your own. Personality profiling is used to gain an understanding of how each of us is different; it gives us the information that allows us to adapt our behaviour and communicate better with others. As an example, if a manager knows that a team member is introverted, they can take steps to ensure that information is presented in a way that allows that person time to go away, digest and analyse the information, rather than expect the immediate response and engagement that would be typical of an extrovert. Particular industries or job types attract certain personality types. Understanding your personality type helps you to market yourself better and be more realistic about options.

What follows is a series of tailored exercises designed to answer these questions:

- Why do you work?
- What do you want from work?
- What sort of person are you?
- What other things do you value in life, and in what proportion?

CAUTION: We recommend you work through the exercises with someone who will ask you the questions and continually check you are being honest with yourself. This should be a trusted person with no vested interest in the outcome, e.g. a careers coach or a reliable colleague. If you do this exercise on your own, the risk is that the version of yourself will be constrained by your lack of awareness of your true capabilities and wider skill set. You have personal 'blind spots' or strengths that you take so much for granted that they are invisible to you. Other people see you differently and more objectively. Working with someone else can be very powerful as they can help you identify aspects of yourself, your work or your achievements that you do not appreciate.

1. KNOWLEDGE AND EXPERIENCE

In this section you'll look at what you have done in your previous work and how it can be described in order to have the greatest impact when you are seeking future employment. Even though it's often said that recruiters are only interested in what you have done most recently, there will be themes and threads running through your career that point to distinct areas of expertise and competence. Knowing what these are allows you to be clear in your opening statement about who you are.

- I am a financial services expert...
- I am a project manager specialising in…
- I coach at director level in organisations…
- I am a management accountant...
- I am an entrepreneur…

Start with a clean sheet of paper, even though a lot of this information may be on your current CV.

1. List all the employers you have worked for, or periods of self-employment, and the job titles you held.
2. Taking each of the jobs in turn, write down the answers to the following questions:

   - What was I responsible for?
   - What did I do in this role?
   - What did I achieve?
   - What am I most proud of in this role?

It's important to remember the 'I' word. This is about you. Avoid describing in too much detail what the company or department did or what projects you were 'involved in' or 'supported'. You're bringing out evidence of the actual work you were doing, what you were asked to do, what you achieved as a result and how you might describe this to a third party. Review your answers until you have come up with a comprehensive list of responsibilities and achievements under each job role.

3. List all the professional memberships, accreditations and qualifications you have achieved since you left full-time education. Include training courses if they are part of, or will lead to, a recognised qualification in your industry, or were provided by a company or body that is highly regarded in your field. It's difficult to be too prescriptive here but what you are looking for is anything that demonstrates a certain level of competence or professionalism to a potential future employer.

4. Finally, repeat steps 2 and 3 above, but this time consider your life *outside* work. What roles or positions do you hold in society or in your local community? What are you responsible for? What have you achieved?

Having completed all four steps above, you should have three lists in front of you:

- **companies I have worked for and my role titles;**
- **jobs I have done in employment or in my personal time, and my respective responsibilities and achievements;**
- **recognised qualifications and certificates of competence.**

Now collate all of the information from this exercise and record it using the following format:

Work history
List your employers and role titles, with dates.
For each role, describe your responsibilities and achievements.
Other activities
As above but in non-paid employment: roles or positions you have held in clubs, societies, professional associations etc.
For each role, describe your responsibilities and achievements.
Education, professional qualifications and memberships
All qualifications, accreditations and memberships that demonstrate competence in a field or sector.

Table 4.1

This is not a CV as such, because a CV is tailored to a particular job. This is a record of you and the work you have done that you can refer to whenever you need to check whether you have the evidence, knowledge or capability to do a future role that you are considering. In Chapter 10, you will develop a CV from this information.

2. SKILLS AND ABILITIES

The first exercise above concerns your employment record and what it says about the capabilities you have. In the second exercise you will delve deeper to uncover what core, transferable skills you have. These skills go with you to any job and are therefore most useful to a future employer. The type of work and the industry sector may change, but your transferable skills will always be available to you.

For this exercise we are indebted to Alison Fair[1], a career counsellor in Maidenhead, Berkshire. She has performed this exercise with thousands of individuals to help them understand what their key skills and abilities are. Alison says:

'By comprehensively deconstructing all your work experiences, achievements and contributions, key skills and abilities begin to emerge – often repeatedly – and underlying patterns and trends can be identified. For example, take someone who – often in their earlier career – was very soon promoted each time they moved on to a new company. This tells me quite a lot about them. They are someone who is able to win the confidence of their employer or manager, they make a good impression, are able to pick up things quickly and make an impact right from the beginning; they are also flexible and adaptable, and able to get stuck in easily. These traits could be key selling points that they could use at interview. They might say, "I am always able to hit the ground running, win trust quickly and make an early impact..." and are able to back up this claim with evidence because it came from an analysis of their actual experience and career history.'

Take a blank sheet of paper, A3 size if you have one. You are going to create a 'mind-map' of you, your employers, jobs and skills. To do this, write your name in the centre of the page, then surround it with the employers you have had. For each employer, list the job titles you held. Make sure you include any voluntary or unpaid roles, e.g. secretary of the local football club. Also include key roles you have held in society, mother or father included (thereby listing *all* of your roles). The job titles form the second layer of the map. The next layer will be the skills you used in each role. The example in Figure 4.1 is for Elizabeth, a health services professional.

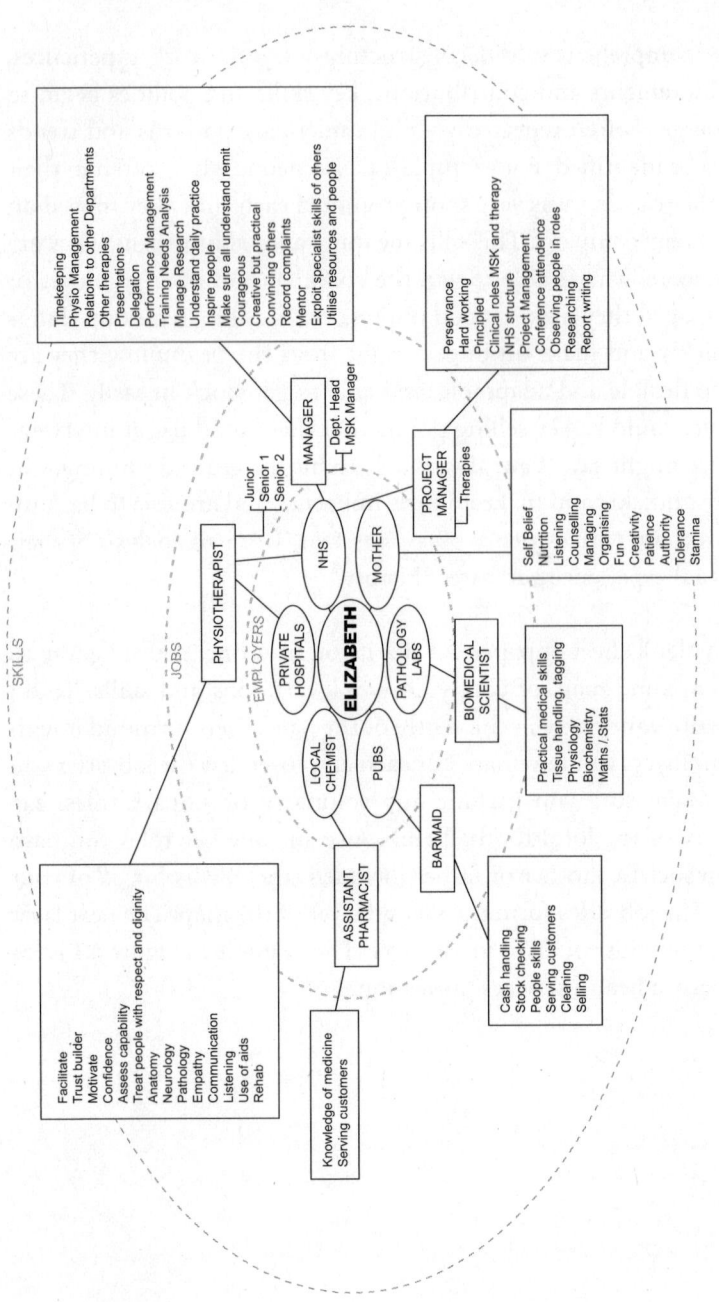

Fig. 4.1 Skills Audit

DERIVING YOUR SKILLS

For each of the jobs on your mind-map spend a few minutes living in the role.

- What did a typical day involve?
- As you think about what you did, keep asking yourself *how* you did it, *why* you did it, and what the outcome was.
- What skills did you need for the task?
- What skills did the role develop?
- If someone were to do your role, what would you say were the key skill requirements to succeed in the way you did?

Keep going until you have described, using lots of 'skills' words, what you did in each of the roles. Some examples of skills words are:

Examples of skills words				
analysed	developed	laid out	organised	sold
assisted	dissected	led	persuaded	supported
automated	educated	listened	planned	sympathised
calculated	entered	managed	prepared	taught
communicated	handled	marketed	presented	trained
created	innovated	motivated	reviewed	treated
deduced	inspired	multitasked	served	verified

Table 4.2

Repeat the exercise for each of the roles you have held, including volunteer and part-time positions.

When you have finished, look at all the skills and job details you have written down and make a list of the words or phrases that are repeated most often which describe the groups of skills you always use in each role. Summarise these as five to 10 core skills that you can take to any role, either as a list or as a new mind-map. These are your 'transferable skills'. Whatever job you do, you always bring these to the table.

As an example, Elizabeth's transferable skills, derived from her mind-map, are shown in Figure 4.2.

Fig. 4.2 Skills Map

Here are two more examples from other industries that might help you to see how you can extract transferable skills from a job title.

Example 1

A highly qualified environmental scientist was made redundant in mid-career after many years with the same company. In discussion with his career coach, he explained how he was the first in his family not only to finish his education, but to go to university and get an undergraduate degree, a masters and a doctorate. He had raised funds for his studies and he was able to repeatedly raise funds for research projects throughout his career. He was recognised at an international level as an expert in his field, conducted training and workshops for others and was asked to speak at international conferences.

By deconstructing his entire career journey, how he did his work and his approach to the projects he worked on, he was able to audit his obvious technical skills and knowledge, but also to point out other core skills that he had overlooked and taken for granted. These skills were instrumental to his personal success:

- great tenacity;
- a refusal to accept barriers;
- inventiveness;
- ingenuity in how he approached problems;
- clarity and simplicity in his thinking and theories;
- clear and concise communication skills; an ability to translate complexity into easily understood lay terms.

By seeing himself as someone with this combination of skills, rather than just an 'environmental scientist', he was able to take a much broader view of what jobs he could apply for.

Example 2

The following is an interview between a career coach and a jobseeker who is a keen sailor. It illustrates how you can extract transferable skills from a hobby.

'So give me an example of a job that you do, in or out of work.'
'I organise and lead a sailing team.'
'What did you have to do to lead the team?'
'I got the team together and assigned tasks for all of them; then over time I improved the team by seeing who was good at what, and I made changes and trained people as required.'
'What did you need to know to do that?'
'An understanding of tasks and an ability to gauge people's potential and to match their skills to each task. I feel I have a natural talent for organising work into tasks and responsibilities and then assigning the right person to each job. Then I have to monitor how they are doing, motivate them and help develop them in those roles. At the same time I have to keep the bigger objective in mind, to race well as a team.'

By performing this exercise, the jobseeker was able to recognise that leading a sailing team meant using a set of transferable people management skills. Those skills are very useful in general and in project management situations in particular. It's no surprise that this individual previously held a project management role in an engineering company.

Analysing your skills in this way has some additional benefits. By disassociating yourself from a role and analysing what skills you used, you can take a much more objective view of the transferable skills you have. These can then be highlighted in a CV or talked about in an interview. This will continue to build confidence in your abilities. You will be able to see, especially as an older worker, how broad a skill base you have. This is of much more interest to a future employer than what is reflected in a simple job title.

Motivated skills

Edgar E. Schein[2] of MIT (Massachusetts Institute of Technology) introduced the term 'career anchors' – the combination of values, beliefs and skills that people use when they are doing well. People tend to stick with these throughout their working lives, hence the use of the term 'anchor'. But some of those skills may not be ones that inspire a person. Someone who has been in the merchant navy for 30 years may have excellent skills in marine navigation but their reason for a career change may be that they are no longer interested in using those skills.

Schein talks about skills that are so natural to us that we are always at our best when using them. He calls them 'motivated skills'. It's essential that you know which ones yours are.

Review your list of transferable skills, established above, and score them on a scale of 1–10 as to how 'motivated' you feel to use each skill. Is it something that you can do well without thinking and that you love doing (score 10/10)? Or is it something you *can* do but would rather not do (score 1/10), or are you somewhere in between? The skills you have rated the highest are what you can call your 'motivated skills'.

3. VALUES AND ASPIRATIONS

'I never felt I fitted in there' is a statement we've all heard. People often reflect on a previous job and conclude that there was some fundamental mismatch between what they expected from the job and what it actually delivered – maybe it was to do with the way their colleagues behaved, how their boss treated them or with what customers demanded. With hindsight this may have been caused by a clash of values – the principles and standards that each of us hold dear. Fairness, honesty, ruthlessness, money as the measure of success, a good balance between work and home life, importance of family; these are all examples of personal values. If there's a big difference between what's important to you and what the company you work for expects, then trouble will ensue.

Your values will have changed over time. What was important to you in your 20s may not be as important to you in your 40s, while other values may now assume a higher importance, for example: those to do with family life or long-term security. This shift in priorities happens gradually over a period of time and, if that time was spent with one employer, the gradual divergence of your values from that of the company can lead to job dissatisfaction. What you strive for is no longer in line with company goals. Your belief that 'They don't value people like me any more' might, in fact, be very true. It's not necessarily the company's fault; it's just that what you want from your work has changed.

Some of us are clear about our values while others find it difficult to be specific and find it easier to identify what they oppose. Either way, your values unconsciously guide your everyday choices of how to live, who to be with, and your work. Ideally, we would all be working for, or with, organisations whose values we share.

In seeking new employment as an older person, an honest appreciation of your values plays a key part in ensuring the work you do is fulfilling and long-lasting. The need to earn an income may be the overriding motivator to take any role that is offered, but if there is a values mismatch with the company or its employees, that employment will not last long and it will not be fulfilling. Career decisions linked to your values are much more powerful than those linked to your needs. Career or job changes later in life can be an opportunity for you to realign your working life with your values, putting you back on a path to success. Assessing your values will assist you in choosing suitable jobs to apply for.

Having a clear understanding of your values can add to your profile on your CV. Phrases that may be relevant to the job you are applying for include: 'a person of honesty and integrity'; 'a strong believer in the principle of sustainable development'; 'a generous and compassionate person who serves his community.'

At interview, you'll be able to answer coded questions about your values, and you can ask intelligent questions about what values the company and your future colleagues hold. In Chapter 11 we will discuss the interviewer's concern: 'Will you fit in?' This question really is about values. What are the values of the person being interviewed and are they compatible with the staff and the organisation? This line of questioning is rarely scientific – interviewers will ask what you do outside work, how you tackle problems, what management style you have, and what people say about you. These questions are designed to unearth clues about what values you hold.

HOW TO DISCOVER YOUR VALUES

This simple exercise will help you articulate your values.

Step 1: Review the general list of values below. If there are others that are not included here, add them. Which ones do you believe in? Think about this in a professional context. *'When at work, I believe in...'* On a clean sheet of paper, note down all the values that apply to you.

Examples of value words		
achievement	freedom	pleasure
advancement	friendships	power and authority
adventure	growth	privacy
affection	having a family	public service
arts	helping other people	purity
capability/competence	helping society	quality of output
challenging problems	honesty	quality of relationships
change and variety	independence	recognition from others

close relationships	influencing others	religious belief
community	inner harmony	reputation
competition	integrity	responsibility
cooperation	intellectual status	security
country	involvement	self-respect
creativity	job stability	serenity
decisiveness	knowledge	sophistication
democracy	leadership	stability
ecological awareness	location	status
economic security	loyalty	supervising others
effectiveness	meaningful work	time freedom
efficiency	merit	trust
ethical practice	money	truth
excellence	nature	wealth
excitement	openness	wisdom
fame and celebrity	order	working under pressure
fast living	personal development	working with others
financial reward	physical challenge	working alone

Table 4.3

Step 2 (optional): If your list from Step 1 has fewer than ten items, proceed straightaway to Step 3. If you have more than ten items, you need to review your list again and select those that are most important. One way of doing this is to use a scoring system. Go down your list and assign points as follows:

- **1 point – a value that you hold to be true some of the time;**
- **2 points – a value that you hold all of the time;**
- **3 points – a value that you absolutely believe in.**

Create a new list consisting only of the items that scored three points. If you have more than ten items, then look at the list again and apply the scoring system to further reduce the list. Keep doing this until you have arrived at ten values or less. Now you can rank the values in order of importance.

Step 3: Ranking the values Now compare each value against the others and decide which one is of higher importance. Let's say your values are:

- Adventure
- Affection
- Recognition from others
- Time freedom
- Independence

- Having a family
- Friendships
- Economic security
- Honesty

Place them on a chart, as we have indicated below. Starting with 'adventure', ask yourself: *'What do I value highest: "adventure" or "having a family"?'* Put a tick next to your choice. Then ask yourself: *'What do I value highest: "adventure" or "affection"?'* Again put a tick next to your choice. Keep going down the list to the end.

Then pick the second item from the top, 'having a family' and ask yourself, *'What do I value highest: "having a family" or "affection"?'* Put a tick against your choice. Find the next item on the list and ask yourself, *'What do I value highest: "having a family" or "friendships"?'* Tick your choice. Keep going down to the bottom, then take the third item in the list and repeat the exercise with all the items below it.

When you have finished you could have a list like this:

Value ranking								
Adventure	✓	✓	✓					
Having a family	✓	✓	✓	✓	✓	✓	✓	
Affection	✓	✓						
Friendships	✓	✓						
Recognition from others	✓	✓	✓	✓	✓			
Economic security	✓	✓	✓	✓				
Time freedom	✓	✓						
Honesty	✓	✓	✓	✓	✓	✓	✓	✓
Independence	✓	✓	✓					

Table 4.4

Rank the values in order of importance. In this example, the values would be ranked as follows, in descending order:

- honesty
- having a family
- recognition from others
- economic security
- adventure
- independence
- affection
- friendships
- time freedom

When you have prepared your list, evaluate your recent jobs against your values. For each job, consider which of your values were respected by the organisation and which were shared with colleagues. You might find there is a correlation between your level of success and fulfilment in the role and a match with your values. As we noted earlier, your values may have changed over time, so don't be surprised if a job you held 30 years ago does not show a good match. On the other hand, if a very recent role shows a poor match, it may help explain why the job wasn't satisfying.

4. PERSONALITY

The final aspect of your self-assessment relates to your personality. What sort of person are you? By this stage in your career you should have a clear idea of the sort of company you like to keep, the way you consider new ideas and take decisions, and whether you prefer to work with materials, processes, or with people. Preferences are a way to specify your personality – what makes you unique. You may describe yourself in broad terms (*I am a very outgoing gregarious person, I am very analytical*) or you may be able to point to a personality indicator you have taken (*I am one of these types: 'ISTJ'*[3]).

Research shows specific personality types tend to be attracted to, and enjoy, certain types of work. If you are considering becoming a self-employed consultant, buying a business, or applying for a job in a caring profession, you may want to reflect on whether you have the type of personality that would thrive in that particular role. We use the words 'tend to' as there are no absolute rules here, and it would be wrong to base a career decision on personality type alone. In fact, having a different personality to the norm certainly doesn't exclude a job possibility – it means you may well be valued for the different perspectives you bring to the role.

An understanding of your personality type will help you to:

- understand why something did not work out for you in the past;
- describe aspects of your personality (in your CV or at interview) that are strengths when working with people or managing teams;
- consider the sort of jobs that suit your personality.

In order to establish your personality type there are a number of options open to you. You may be able to call on a number of personality profile tests that you have taken in the past. Reports will be fairly accurate as long as they were done while you were in employment and they were based on your real experience of work. Two personality preference or type tests that are widely used to predict performance at work are the Myers Briggs Personality Indicator (MBTI) and the DISC profile (Dominance, Influence, Steadiness, and Conscientiousness). (See the Resources section at the end of the book.)

You can pay to undergo a specific personality test. If so, pick one that is part of a careers advice or coaching service, so that the information produced is directly relevant to a job search. For example, a career planning assessment from Proteus, a UK career management consultancy[4], will cover your work style preferences as well as highlight the job types and roles suited to your personality.

Finally, you can go online and get a free or low-cost personality assessment. Again, look for one that is part of a career or job-search package so that the output data is relevant to your situation. A useful tool is Adult Directions[5], an online resource from Loughborough

University that uses work-related interests, skills and desired occupation level to identify suitable careers.

Mapping personality types to job roles requires access to research data. You can either refer to books like *Do What You Are*[6] by Paul D. Tieger and Barbara Barron-Tieger or ensure that the guidance you receive as part of a paid-for test provides you with the information you need. The list of job types and roles that match your personality may not, at first, appear to offer prospects of a successful career change in the short term. They are often food for thought when considering future career options. For example, if your personality indicator tells you that your personality is ideally suited to a job in coaching or mentoring, you can seek management roles where a degree of coaching is required, rather than making a total career change.

SUMMARY: BRINGING IT ALL TOGETHER

You have worked through your self-assessment and now have a very good idea of the experience and track record you can point to as evidence of your capability. You know your 'transferable skills' – the ones that you bring to any work or social situation. You also know your 'motivated skills' – the ones that you use with passion. Your values give you vital clues about the sort of work environment in which you thrive. The work to which you are ideally suited will match your personality.

Equipped with this information, you're set to market yourself to employers, become self-employed or choose a business to manage. The next step is to consider which options are realistic and turn your assessment into a personal strategy and action plan.

CREATE A WINNING STRATEGY

5

THE WORK FUNNEL

ASSESSMENT – Chapter 4
Personality, Skills,
Values, Experience, Capabilities

STRATEGY – Chapter 5
Long-term goals
Context
Options

ACTION – Chapter 6
Decisions
Plan
Resources
Search

ACTION TOOLS & SKILLS
Networking
Business Planning
Interviews
Applications

OUTCOMES
Jobs
Interim
Portfolio
Consultant
Own Business

You've assessed your skills, capabilities, personality and values. That was the analysis stage. Now you can take that information and consider it in the context of your current situation and future aspirations, and then develop a strategy for the future. Finding your next job or role is a process. You may feel your strategy at the moment is just to get an income, but you need to think about your longer-term future. The days of a safe, secure pension at 60 are fast disappearing, and so the nature and type of work that you do could make all the difference to how your retirement plans play out. This is the hub of the book; it's where you start looking forward and preparing the grounds for decisions that will dictate what you do for the next few decades.

We've already mentioned 'career capital', the experience, skills and qualifications you have gained so far. It's what employers look at when deciding on your capabilities: the work that you did in your 20s and 30s is now shaping your future options. It's easy to think that your choices are limited and regret that you didn't take certain opportunities. But you are where you are; if you're in your 40s or 50s, you still have 15 to 25 working years left in you. There is still plenty of scope to build up career capital that you can trade on in the future. Any strategy you create now is much more likely to be successful, given your enhanced self-awareness.

A winning career strategy has the same elements as a business plan: it begins with a vision and mission statement, defining your goals and ambitions and how you intend to achieve them. You'll consolidate your thinking in terms of a SWOT analysis: a list of the internal Strengths and Weaknesses of your current position, and the external Opportunities and Threats that you might encounter.

Note: If you have an interest in self-employment options, before proceeding further you may want to review Chapters 12 to 14 and consider the self-employment alternatives. You can then return to this chapter to create your strategy.

HAVE A LONG-TERM GOAL

We all have dreams of what we will do one day, whether in retirement or later in our working life. How do we turn these dreams into reality?

As Stephen Covey stated in his book *The Seven Habits of Highly Effective People*, 'start with the end in mind'. The first step in deciding your overall strategy is to think about your long-term aim – where you want to be living, what you'd like to be doing, who you want to be with and how much money you want or need. Evidence shows that people who spend time thinking clearly about their specific goals and aspirations will achieve more and enjoy greater fulfilment than those who don't give them proper consideration. Without an aspiration to be doing something different in five or ten years' time, chances are you will be doing something very similar to what you are doing now. If you want to make any changes, especially in terms of work, it's useful to define your long-term goal.

DEVELOP A VISION AND MISSION

To continue with the business plan analogy, the first step is to develop a 'vision' and a 'mission'. Your vision is your long-term goal: what you are striving for, or, as some people see it, your purpose in life. Your mission is the strategy used to achieve your vision. Some people find that their vision and mission have always been clear. For others, it's taken a battering through the pressures of work, family and personal constraints. Now is the time to resurrect your vision and act upon it. This could be the most powerful call to action you will experience.

The simple but powerful exercise below is a good start towards planning your long-term goals. It's a visualisation technique widely used in coaching. You're asked to imagine that you are already at the end of your career and are now looking back, reflecting on how you achieved your success. It requires you to think carefully, so find some quiet, quality time to do it. Initially, perform the exercise alone. Then you might want to repeat it with someone who will play a key role in your strategy, such as a partner or friend. They can help you develop the details. But be aware that anyone you invite will have their own vested interests.

THE RETIREMENT PARTY GAME

Imagine you are at your retirement party. Your time of working for a living has ended – from now on you do what you like when you like.

Your personal, family and financial goals have been met. You're surrounded by people who have contributed to your joy: a mix of friends, family, and business colleagues. You feel a buzz in the room. The windows to the terrace are open and a sea breeze gently stirs the curtains. The smell of the sea reminds you of the boat trip you have planned for everyone tomorrow. Nearby, the chef is just getting the barbecue going. As you stand up to make a welcome speech, everyone is enjoying their drinks and looking at you in admiration. You look around with a warm smile of contentment.

You give a short thank-you speech and enjoy the applause. Imagine the speech. What do you say?

As you step down off the stage, an old friend walks up to you and says, 'Great to see you. When we last met, you seemed to be struggling a bit. How come you're so happy now?'

So you tell him:

- why you are so content;
- where you are living;
- what you do;
- who you share your life with;
- what your last job was;
- why you are retiring;
- what you are proud of achieving;
- who the people in the room are and what they mean to you.

This is your vision. Write it down – it's where you want to go.

The old friend is fascinated. 'It's good to see you so happy. How did you do it?'

You tell him: 'Well, all those years ago I was made redundant and I decided to...'

Now fill in the details as best you can as if you were telling the story at your retirement party.

- What did you do that proved to be a great decision?
- Who did you work for?

- What work did you do?
- What financial actions did you take?
- How did you bring your family, partners or close friends with you?
- What skills did you pick up on the way – personal as well as technical?
- What big breaks did you get? How did you position yourself to take advantage of them?
- What difficulties did you face?
- How did you overcome them?
- Who helped you on the way?
- What were the critical decisions you took?

This is your mission. It's how you achieved your vision. Write it down.

Work on your vision and your mission until you feel comfortable with the descriptions. It may be worth repeating the exercise with someone you trust. Do this over several days or weeks to tease out all your intuitions about your dream and how to achieve it.

FACTOR IN THE CONSTRAINTS

Now that you're clear on your vision and mission, it's important to look at your limitations and factor them into your long-term strategy. Age is one of them, but it can also open up lots of opportunities. Consider how the assets that age brings can be used strategically. You have considerable career capital. A career in your 50s will be built on the experience and contacts you developed in your 40s, and the same can be said for those in their 60s about the work they did in their 50s. It's always possible to build on past achievements.

You'll also need to consider the environment you are in, the people you are with, the location you can work in and your financial constraints. Your environment is not static – it changes as time passes. Take children for example: an 11-year-old child is very dependent on you; a 14-year-old less so, and a 21-year-old may be financially independent. Over the next two or three decades your family's reliance upon you may radically change. And your responsibility for children may be replaced by an obligation to ageing parents. In order to consider your environment over the longer term, it's useful to draw a timeline diagram showing the key milestones for the next 10–15 years.

To construct the timeline, first list the key people, milestones and commitments in your life. For example, your list might include: partner, children, son, daughter, step-daughter, parents, mortgage, investments, partner's parents, pension, inheritances, etc. Next, map out the ages and significant milestone events for these people or things over the coming years (choose a timescale that makes sense for you). In particular, note any financial or time requirements. Table 5.1 is a simple example.

The table shows the age progression of a couple now in their 40s with two young children and ageing parents. Also shown is an investment that matures in 2016, and a mortgage that at the current rate will be paid off in 2023. Make up your own table and include as much relevant detail as you can.

If you repeat this for all the people or things in your life in a table format like this, then you can begin to see a future timeline of your life. When will you need more finance? When are you likely to have more time on your hands? When might you need to be caring for others? Is there a time, as in the example above, when your children leave home and your ageing parents require additional healthcare? Looking at the whole picture over the next 15 years, what conclusions do you draw about:

- how long you will have to work?
- when you will need to have more flexible working arrangements?
- how much income you will need?
- what other opportunities present themselves, such as inheritances?
- where will you be to be located in five or ten years' time?
- what other opportunities exist?

At this point, it's worth refining your vision and mission statements, bearing in mind what the above forward-looking exercise has revealed to you.

Age in:	2010	2011	2012	2013	2014	2015	2016	2017	2018	2019	2020	2021	2022	2023	2024
Me	44	45	46	47	48	49	50	51	52	53	54	55	56	57	58
Partner	45	46	47	48	49	50	51	52	53	54	55	56	57	58	59
My mother	78	79	80	81	82	83	84	85	86	87	88	89	90	91	92
My father	76	77	78	79	80	81	82	83	84	85	86	87	88	89	90
Partner's mother	72	73	74	75	76	77	78	79	80	81	82	83	84	85	86
Partner's father	73	74	75	76	77	78	79	80	81	82	83	84	85	86	87
Son	7	8	9	10	11	12	13	14	15	16	17	18	19	20	21
Daughter	11	12	13	14	15	16	17	18	19	20	21	22	23	24	25
Milestones			Daughter starts secondary school		Son starts secondary school		Investment matures		Daughter starts university			Son starts university; Daughter into work		Mortgage paid off	

Table 5.1 Sample Timeline with Milestones

WHAT ARE YOUR OPTIONS?

Before going any further with a future plan based on your dreams and goals, take a look around and see what is realistically achievable. Be specific: what jobs can you do and what is available? What salaries are on offer for those jobs? Is the remuneration a realistic option for you? If your self-assessment points to employment in a new sector, how much does the position pay and how long does it take to retrain?

Sometimes we have to accept that there are many dream options but there are only one or two realistic ones. With a list of options to hand, you'll need to do some research. Your first port of call should be your network. This is a perfect opportunity to contact people and ask for information and guidance – but not a job. Most people are open to talking about what they do and discussing opportunities in their sector, as long as they are not under the impression that you expect them to find you a job. Network far and wide, and don't forget that the best sources of information are the contacts of your contacts (see Chapter 7). As well as your personal network, look at business networking events, and industry seminars and exhibitions. Where do the 'great and good' of the industry meet?

When it comes to researching specifics about roles, much of what you need is found online. A good online resource is Adult Directions, mentioned in Chapter 4. You can also seek advice from a number of specific sources for adult careers guidance. In the UK, Next Step (**https://nextstep.direct.gov.uk**) is a publicly funded service which offers access to online resources and telephone support as well as face-to-face meetings with an adviser.

It might be worth speaking to a friendly recruitment agent who works in the industry you are considering. Where are the predicted growth areas? What sort of people do they place? What particular skills and qualifications do employers seek? What are the typical rates of pay for contract or permanent work? These are all questions a good recruitment agent should be able to answer, if you can get a meeting or have a telephone conversation.

Finally, if you have a very well-defined job target, try researching specific companies and niche industries. For instance, if you want a job in the marine industry in the UK, the British Marine Federation can provide a list of companies operating in the sector, and you'll probably find that only a few companies match your criteria.

WEIGH UP THE RISKS

A useful way to assess options is to consider them in terms of risk. If you have been employed as an accountant in the energy sector for most of your life, then the lowest risk option is to find a similar role in the same sector. A medium risk option would be to remain in accountancy but move into self-employment or into a new sector. You could stay in the energy sector but use your accountancy skills to get a business or operational management role. The highest risk approach would be to decide that accountancy is not for you, and retrain as an engineer in another sector, such as technology.

This table summarises the different approaches:

	Same sector	New sector
Same type of work	Low risk	Medium risk
New type of work	Medium risk	Highest risk

Table 5.2

Any of these moves are possible, but starting a new type of work in a new industry sector would likely be the biggest challenge. Table 5.3 opposite shows what strategies you might employ and what opportunities might arise, depending on your strategic choice. In two categories – new sector and new type of work – you would need to convince an employer that your transferable skills would make it possible for them to employ you.

Draw a similar table of options if you are considering self-employment, or entrepreneurship, as shown in Table 5.4. In general, the lowest risk approach when deciding to move into self-employment would be to work in a field that you know well. Otherwise, not only would you need to gain knowledge about a new sector, at the same time you would also need to learn all about being self-employed.

	Same sector	New sector
Same type of work	Strategy: Refocus. What am I really good at? Can I specialise? Opportunity: Promotion, deepening expertise, higher responsibility.	Strategy: Redirect skills. Apply expertise in different industry. Opportunity: Growth, gain new experience, develop new contacts.
New type of work	Strategy: Use contacts and industry knowledge to change roles. Opportunity: Gain new skills and experience (career capital).	Strategy: Career change, retrain for something new. Opportunity: Fresh start.

Table 5.3

A lower risk approach would be to take on freelance consultancy work initially, get familiar with self-employment, and then train later in an additional field so as to broaden the scope of your consultancy base.

	Same field of work	New field of work
Employee	Low risk	Medium risk. Need to learn a new job or new sector.
Self-employed	Medium risk. Need to establish a client base.	Highest risk. Can you learn about this field of work _and_ establish a client base at the same time?

Table 5.4

Given the options you are considering, what level of risk are you entertaining? Does your situation (financial and otherwise) make this level of risk acceptable? If you have taken a large redundancy payment and can afford not to earn for a couple of years, it may be worth retraining and setting up as a consultant in a new field. Your options are always greater than you think and evaluating them in terms of risk is a useful way of determining what your next steps should be.

SWOT ANALYSIS

Any good business review will include an analysis of the business's Strengths and Weaknesses, which are internal, and its Opportunities and Threats, which are external. In career terms it's useful to summarise your thoughts in a SWOT table, as follows:

Strengths	Weaknesses
What are your key skills, experiences, qualifications and achievements (career capital)?	When considering your career options, what skills, qualifications or attributes do you lack at this time?
What factors (financial, geographical, health, contacts, family) will work in your favour in your job search, now and in the long term?	Where can you seek advice or training to address these areas of weakness?
Opportunities	**Threats**
What realistic job and career opportunities would allow you to work towards achieving your vision?	What life situations will potentially prevent you from achieving your vision?
What support networks can you use to explore these?	What external factors would prevent you from getting the job or role you are seeking?
Which people will be useful allies in your job search and how will you engage them?	How can you mitigate these risks or plan ahead for their occurrence?

Table 5.5

THE WAY FORWARD

You should now be able to answer the following questions with clarity and confidence.

- What industry sectors do I have experience in and what transferable skills do I have that make me employable?
- What type of role am I best suited to do? Project manager, accountant, counsellor, managing director?
- Where do I want/need to work? In a specific country or city?
- What are my salary objectives? How much money do I need to earn per year and for how long?
- What type of employment am I looking for: self-employment, contract, temporary, interim, fixed-term, permanent, franchise, voluntary or a combination of the above?

Once you have firm answers to these questions, it's also useful to note down the answers to two supplementary questions that will be useful as you execute your strategy.

- What support do I have access to: networks, partners, mentors, advisers, sponsors, who can help me achieve my goals?
- What gaps exist in my skill set or experience that I can fill as soon as possible through education, training courses or voluntary work?

Having considered all these questions, now create a one page document that summarises your strategy, being sure to include an answer to each question. As a final step before committing to your strategy, it's a good idea to do a reality check with someone close to you – your spouse, friend, business partner or career coach.

A WINNING STRATEGY

In our work with jobseekers, we've discovered that people with a clear and well-thought out concept can do better than those with superior qualifications but who lack clarity in their objectives. For an example, see Matt Williams' story (p.220). Matt visited the Job Club and told everyone he was convinced that his way forward was to set up as an independent digital printer. Other club members cautioned against it, warning that printing is a competitive market and questioning whether he had the skills and experience to do it. Confident in his vision, he sought independent business advice, found a market niche, and within months was established as an independent printer. The clarity of his vision, the confidence in his own approach and his willingness to take on advice in areas in which he felt weak, was enough to get him started. For Matt, it was a winning strategy. When others questioned it, he was able to come back to a secure and confident position: *This is what I really want to do, and I know it is realistic to achieve my goals if I proceed this way.*

Your winning strategy may take time to execute. Be flexible in how you implement it and you'll find it is your passport to a fulfilling career in later life. Your belief that you are finally doing the right thing will carry you through the obstacles that any job search presents.

In the next chapter we'll show you how to break your goals down into smaller steps, so that you have an effective action plan.

MAKING YOUR STRATEGY WORK

CHAPTER

6

THE WORK FUNNEL

ASSESSMENT – Chapter 4
Personality, Skills,
Values, Experience, Capabilities

STRATEGY – Chapter 5
Long-term goals
Context
Options

ACTION – Chapter 6
Decisions
Plan
Resources
Search

ACTION TOOLS & SKILLS
Networking
Business Planning
Interviews
Applications

OUTCOMES
Jobs
Interim
Portfolio
Consultant
Own Business

You've created a strategy you think will bring you success. But what exactly will you do tomorrow to begin your work search? Turning a strategy into action involves commitment: thinking through in detail what you will do, how and when you will do it; taking decisions and committing to action. It means having a plan.

The following story was told to Liam by Adrian Moorhouse, who won a gold medal for Britain at the 1988 Olympics. Adrian recounted how, when he was a junior swimmer, a coach helped him set his sights on achieving his dream.

'What's an Olympic race winning time?' the coach asked.

'About six minutes and 30 seconds,' Adrian replied.

'What's your time for that distance now?'

'Six minutes and 45 seconds.'

'So the next Olympics are three years away. Can you manage a 15-second improvement by then?'

Adrian thought about it before replying, 'Well, I don't know...I think so.'

'Let's look at it another way,' the coach said. 'There are 150 weeks of training between now and then. Do you think you can swim one-tenth of a second faster every week between now and then?'

'Of course, definitely, yes, I'm sure I can do that.'

'Ok, so we have a plan,' said the coach.

A plan has to have goals. This story illustrates the difference between 'performance' goals and 'outcome' goals. The outcome goal was to win an Olympic medal. By breaking it down into a series of achievable steps, Adrian set performance goals. You can do the same with job-seeking. Your goal as defined in Chapter 5 is a well-defined outcome goal. It's something specific and realistic, you know why you want it, it's described in language that means something to you and it inspires you to action.

PERFORMANCE GOALS

It can be daunting to face your outcome goal every day, knowing it may be months before it is achieved. This is where performance goals come in. They measure the activities you undertake to achieve your outcome goal. You have more control over your achievement with a performance goal than you do with an outcome goal. Performance goals help you redefine success. When job-seeking, it is a trap to measure success only by whether or not you find work. It's far more useful to define success as the completion of specific tasks and actions that lead to work.

In subsequent chapters we explain how to network with a purpose, contact head-hunters and recruitment agents, post your CV selectively in response to job advertisements, send speculative applications to identified companies, rehearse answers to interview questions, and prepare for interviews by practising. You can set performance goals around all of these tasks. Your performance goals need to be very specific. It pays to revisit them on a frequent basis, at least once a month.

Your plan will have two phases: preparation and marketing. Here are some examples of performance goals for preparation:

- by [date] I will have completed my CV;
- by [date] I will have identified two industry sectors where my skills are applicable;
- by [date] I will have identified five recruitment consultants operating in those sectors;
- by [date] I will have defined what my proposition is to potential clients for my consultancy services;
- every morning I will review jobs available on my chosen job search websites.

Some performance goals for your marketing phase:

- by [date] I will have contacted four people in my industry;
- every week I will apply for at least three jobs online;
- every week I will contact four new people to do with my job search;
- every week I will attend at least one professional networking event;
- by [date] I will e-mail an introductory CV to at least five agencies;
- by [date] I will send a speculative application to at least 20 companies in my chosen sector.

The marketing phase is open-ended because it goes on until you find the work that you want. You can keep yourself motivated and inspired during this phase by having performance goals that, when achieved, provide you with a sense of making progress even though the outcome goal of 'work' has not yet been realised.

A DAILY ROUTINE

As a jobseeker, you are your own boss. We recommend you establish some basic routines. For example, you might start every Monday morning by setting targets for the number of calls to make and CVs to send, as well as planning your networking and other meetings. Then at the end of the week, review what you did and, if necessary, change your plan for the following week. Your routine might involve regular time slots for:

- checking e-mails;
- looking at job boards;
- applying for jobs online;
- sending letters;
- making phone calls; and
- researching companies.

A SUPPORT NETWORK

Many jobseekers say that one of their biggest challenges is maintaining the support of partners and family. If the only measure of your progress is whether or not you have a job, your loved ones can be disheartened even though you are making progress. With a job-search plan you can report to them. You can show that you are working hard, ticking the tasks off the lists from your plan, and you're celebrating small successes.

What other useful people can you enrol in your plan? By enrolling we mean that you let them know what you're doing, and you report back to them on your progress so they can offer positive encouragement as well as guidance or advice. These people might be key network contacts who can be brutally honest with you about how well you are doing. You might consider using a career coach or careers adviser.

KEEPING YOUR PLAN ALIVE

Don't make a plan only to file it away as another task done. Your plan needs to live with you; it needs to be a visible constant reminder of the realistic targets that motivate you. Print it, draw it, write it on a flipchart, have it pop up on your laptop every day or pin a copy in your diary: do something to keep the plan in front of you on a daily basis.

STARTING AND STAYING COMMITTED

All actions beget reactions. Sometimes the biggest obstacle to starting your work search is the fear of rejection. Making applications will result in rejection; some networking calls won't appear useful; research into new career options could lead to dead ends. You may unconsciously feel it's better to prevent negative consequences by simply avoiding taking action, or you may have experienced enough rejection already. When your actions are driven by a decision to execute your plan, all rejections become part of the route to success. In our experience, successful jobseekers make a plan at some stage to focus on achieving one outcome goal. Rejections and obstacles are overcome with persistence, and then things start to go your way.

'Until one is committed, there is hesitancy, the chance to draw back. Concerning all acts of initiative (and creation), there is one elementary truth that ignorance of which kills countless ideas and splendid plans: that the moment one definitely commits oneself, then Providence moves too. All sorts of things occur to help one that would never otherwise have occurred. A whole stream of events issues from the decision, raising in one's favour all manner of unforeseen incidents and meetings and material assistance, which no man could have dreamed would have come his way. Whatever you can do, or dream you can do, begin it. Boldness has genius, power, and magic in it. Begin it now.'

(widely attributed to Goethe)

SUMMARY

A plan gives you a reason to take meaningful action on a daily basis. It can be highly motivating on those days when nothing seems to be worth doing. If you're feeling down, you can call on actions that you agreed when you were in a more resourceful state. You can reflect on achievements and celebrate success. A plan helps you affirm to yourself and others that you are making progress even when the outcome goal seems distant.

A word of warning: don't be trapped by your plan. If an aspect of the plan is not working, change it. While it is important to follow a strategy and plan for enough time to give it a chance of success, be wise enough to recognise when a plan isn't working. Sending five applications and getting rejected does not mean that your job-hunting is doomed to fail. Sending 200 applications for a certain type of work and getting no response signals the need for a different approach. It is only by regularly reviewing what you are doing and assessing how effective it is that you will know if your plan is working.

And allow yourself to dream – sometimes the unforeseen consequences of following your plan can be more fruitful than the intended outcome.

3

Develop Your Network and Upgrade Your Skills

NETWORKING OR NOT WORKING

CHAPTER 7

THE WORK FUNNEL

ASSESSMENT – Chapter 4
Personality, Skills,
Values, Experience, Capabilities

STRATEGY – Chapter 5
Long-term goals
Context
Options

ACTION – Chapter 6
Decisions
Plan
Resources
Search

ACTION TOOLS & SKILLS
Networking
Business Planning
Interviews
Applications

OUTCOMES
Jobs
Interim
Portfolio
Consultant
Own Business

SIX DEGREES OF SEPARATION

In his 1990 play *Six Degrees of Separation*, American playwright John Guare described the concept that if someone you know can be said to be one 'degree' of separation away from you, and people they know can be said to be two 'degrees' away from you, then anyone on planet Earth is no more than six 'degrees' (steps, or connections) of separation from you. Under this principle, anyone you need to meet in order to make your search for a job or work successful is no more than six connections away from you, and probably a lot less.

This degree of connectedness is best demonstrated by online networking sites such as LinkedIn. LinkedIn tells Liam that he 'knows' nearly five million people. This means there are five million people who are less than three connections away from him, so he could ask one of his contacts to introduce him through one of their contacts. This is an indicator of how vast our personal networks can be. Take another example: at a meeting of the Job Club, a group of mature jobseekers worked out that, between them, they were only three connections away from Bill Gates of Microsoft and every UK rock star.

The challenge is not to accumulate long lists of contacts; rather it is to focus your energy on those people who are of greatest value to your search for employment. This chapter will show you how. We'll examine what networking is all about, how you can build your network – whether in work or out of it – and provide guidance from the 'coalface' for successful networking.

WHAT IS NETWORKING?

Networking is the art of building alliances. You are networking when you are developing relationships that help you to realise your goals. Social networking is investing time with people you like. Business networking is making contact with people who are or can become your suppliers, partners or customers, or who can introduce you to useful contacts. In a job-seeking context, networking simply means maximising the chance that someone with a vacancy will learn that you are available.

Most of our daily activities involve interacting with other people. At what point does it become networking? In this book, three types of activity are called networking.

1. Staying in touch with people you know (socially or professionally) in order to assist them or to obtain their assistance.
2. Identifying people you want to meet (e.g. a potential employer or client) and then using your existing contacts to get a personal introduction.
3. Building and expanding your contacts by attending events such conferences and seminars.

Some would identify a fourth type of networking as 'serendipity': making connections completely by chance that turn out to be useful. Since there is no method for dealing with luck, we will discuss the first three.

Networking can take place face-to-face, on the phone, one-to-one, one-to-many, online or offline. You are networking when you:

- attend a business seminar;
- meet and greet at a parents' evening;
- make a presentation at any gathering (business or social);
- establish connections using an online networking group;
- make social contact in an office with people outside your department;
- organise a local community event;
- go to a trade show.

Networking is NOT:

- cold-calling people to ask for assistance;
- asking friends for a job.

In business it's often said that 'people buy from people'. When networking, it's important to be yourself, because that's what another person is buying into: you and what you have to offer. It's also the best way to develop a useful and lasting relationship. As you go through this chapter we will review how you present yourself and your history, and discuss techniques that will make your network perform better.

AGE IS ON YOUR SIDE

Why? First, because of the number of years you have been around, you probably have many more contacts than you might expect. These contacts have seen the work you can do and the results you are able to produce. They are your advocates. 'I knew Helen many years ago at ABC Ltd, she's worth seeing', or 'You should contact John, he's really good at that kind of work' is the sort of recommendation you might receive, even from people you may have long forgotten.

Second, as an experienced person seeking employment, it's sometimes difficult to match your unique mix of experience and capabilities to a specific job description. This is when a personal introduction can place you in front of a potential employer (or someone connected to a potential employer). Over lunch, coffee, or a drink, you then have the chance to sell your skills away from the pressure of a formal interview and without having your CV rated against the competition.

KEEPING AIR IN THE BALLOON

John was made redundant from his job at ACME plc after 15 years' employment. On his outplacement course, one message was drummed through loud and clear: *70 per cent of new jobs are discovered through networking*. But how do you network? No one made that obvious. John carried a positive attitude into his job search: he called people he used to work with years ago, contacted old friends who hadn't been in touch for a long time, turned up at his professional body's monthly meetings – he even went to a local business networking event and gave a strong pitch to 25 strangers. But he got nowhere – his old colleagues feigned interest in his situation; they offered sympathy and vague promises to 'keep an eye out for you'. Networking events intimidated John because everyone introduced themselves as successful and busy. So he gave up. Four weeks after starting his job search, his networking came to an end. What next?

Lisa was made redundant from a position she had held for three years in the pharmaceuticals industry. Throughout her career she had been a regular attendee at a twice-yearly social/business meeting run by professionals in her industry. Lisa was known among people in her circle of work-related friends as someone always ready to give advice and support, and she was active in her community as a governor at her local school. A handful of fellow students on her MBA course had gone on to fairly senior positions in other organisations and Lisa made a point of attending the annual reunion party, despite the demands on her personal and business diaries. She also became active with online networking sites, getting in touch with long-lost colleagues.

When news of her redundancy hit, she made a few calls to her closest friends in the industry to update them on her situation. Over the next few months she gradually contacted all the people in her network, probably as often as she had been doing previously, but each time ensuring they were aware that she was looking for work. A fellow school governor knew someone at his workplace who was able to give Lisa a three-month consultancy contract. While she was there, an old work colleague contacted her to say her former employer's main competitor had a vacancy that suited her and the MD had enquired if she would be interested.

What's the difference between John and Lisa? Throughout her career, Lisa invested time and effort in building and maintaining a network, whereas John sought only to use his network when he needed it. A professional network is like a hot air balloon: only by constantly keeping it inflated can we count on it when required; left untended, the balloon slowly deflates of its own accord. An unfortunate truth is that the longer you are in secure employment with one employer, the less prepared you are to network for a new job.

If you are like John and you find yourself with no network to speak of, take heart, all is not lost. Everyone has a network of some social and business contacts and, like John, you only need a bit more thought and effort to make it work for you.

BEFORE YOU LEAVE: 10 WAYS TO ENHANCE YOUR NETWORK FOOTPRINT WHILE STILL IN EMPLOYMENT

1. Seek opportunities to represent your company at meetings with suppliers, customers and partners. Make and develop contacts in those groups.
2. Build meaningful business relationships at work. Your colleagues, whether junior or senior to you now, may go on to hold positions in other companies where they may be of use to you. Playing internal politics, whether it comes naturally or not, is often as simple as introducing yourself to people. In some organisations the value of networking internally is recognised and formally encouraged, while in others it is more sporadic.
3. Develop outside business interests without compromising your work. For example, a facilities manager at a major corporate could have a financial interest in an air-conditioning supply company, or an IT support manager could develop a specialised online service in the evenings and at weekends.
4. Attend meetings of your professional body; write articles for publication; write and reply to letters; get your name known in the profession.
5. Attend external training courses where delegates from other companies will be present.
6. Maintain contact with colleagues from earlier stages of your career.
7. Seek networking opportunities within your local community: schools, faith groups and sports clubs. This could mean taking a position of responsibility such as a governor or coach, or simply helping with organisation.

8. Offer free services to organisations you support.
9. Attend industry fairs and events.
10. Never pass up an opportunity to make a connection with someone, however fruitless it appears at the time.

STARTING TO NETWORK

It's sometimes difficult to know where to begin. You are almost certainly already making and maintaining connections with other people, which is a form of networking. But when it comes to networking with a purpose, a more structured approach is required.

In Chapters 4 and 5 we covered the importance of knowing your own strengths and weaknesses and deciding how to position yourself for presentation to potential employers. It's essential to be clear about these before you start networking. Being certain of what you can offer and, therefore, who is most likely to respond will increase your confidence and guide you in the right direction.

The following four-step exercise will begin establishing who is in your network today, and how relationships can be used to your advantage.

Step 1. Make a list of all the people you know in these groupings, or others you can think of:

- friends and family;
- work/business contacts;
- sports and leisure;
- professional groups;
- voluntary work/faith groups;
- school, college and/or university contacts;
- online contacts.

In each category, ask yourself what other groups of people you know. For example, under university, what courses did you attend? List each one as a potential source of contacts.

Add more detail to the list, naming the groups and, in each one, listing the names of the individuals concerned. Some people find it best to do this as a mind-map, as shown in Figure 7.1.

When creating your list or mind-map, it's important to name anyone with whom you have a connection, without making judgements such as: 'I'm not sure he'll talk to me', or 'I haven't spoken to her for years'.

Once you have completed the list, ask a friend to help you remember any additional contacts you may have. Some connections may be tenuous, but at least they are listed. This is your 'first-level network'.

Step 2. Now start asking yourself, 'Who do these people know?' and add those people or groups to the list or map. For example: an ex-colleague has moved to another employer; now he knows a group of people at that company – add those to your list. If it's not possible to add names, list them as a group, for example: 'employees at company X'. Do this for all the contacts on your map or list. This is your 'second-level network' of people you can contact through someone in your network: two degrees of separation.

Step 3. Next, it's time to assess your network and begin to consider how you can make it work for you. Here are two examples:

If you have a specific goal in mind, such as a career move into the sports and leisure sector by targeting companies based in the southwest of the UK, go through your network list and identify the top ten persons or groups who are either in this sector or who have a connection to someone in it, as well as any preferred companies. Is there a friend who knows someone in this sector – perhaps an ex-colleague who moved there – or a college you went to that runs a degree course for the sector you are targeting? Sometimes it may help to share this list with a friend or colleague and ask them to help you identify anything that is not obvious to you. Make a list of these top ten people or possible connections through your network.

If you have a much more general goal, for example, you are considering your next move after 20 years in the IT industry, make a list of ten people who may assist you in taking the next step. They might be others who have made a similar choice, or people in industries or sectors with roles you have always found interesting.

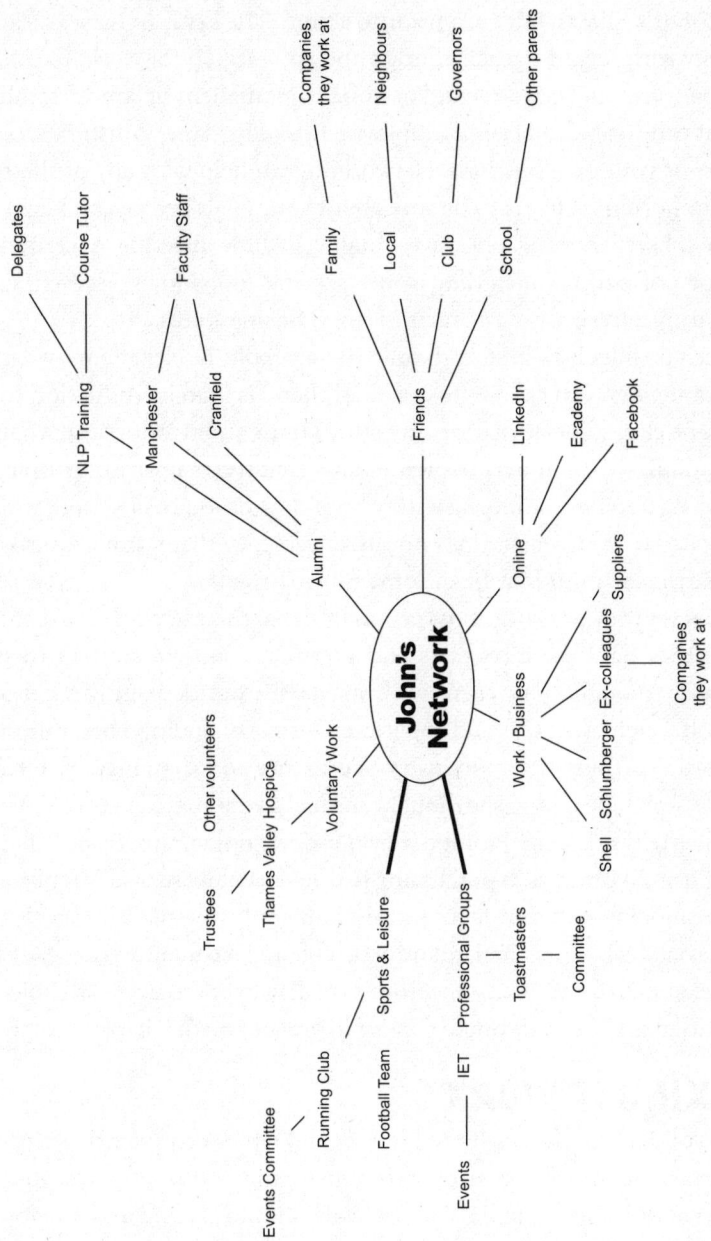

Figure 7.1 Network Example

Step 4. It's time to put your list into action. The key is to have a clear strategy with regard to each contact and your search for work. In this context work can be a job – paid or unpaid, permanent or contract, full or part time – or it can be self-employment as a freelance consultant or as part of your own business. Networking can help with any of these – the important thing is to be sure about your goals before you begin. For a jobseeker, your objectives might include meeting a certain category of people, including some specific individuals, as well as generating a fresh set of contacts in a new business area.

Next, consider how best to contact these people. Be clear about what you want when you call, write or e-mail them. Is it an introduction to someone else, some advice, or a meeting? If it's an introduction, what can you offer them in return? Remember that the majority of people, when asked to help someone with whom they have a connection, will gladly do so as long as it does not inconvenience them unnecessarily and particularly if it may be of some future benefit.

Whatever your objective, most people find that this exercise helps them realise they have more contacts and potential connections than they previously thought. One client we worked with was despairing (after a long job search using CVs and application forms) of finding a new role in purchasing in the maritime industry. She was new to the country in which she was searching and so she thought she had a very limited network. We drew her network map. Prompted by our questioning, she recalled that one of her old contacts in purchasing had kept a database of all suppliers to the shipping industry. It took two phone calls to establish that this private database was up to date and accessible and it contained over 4,000 names. At a stroke she had gone from a small network to having a choice of thousands in her network to contact in order to further her job search.

MAKING IT WORK

Once you have decided who to contact and why to contact them, it's important to move forward with a plan that both achieves your objective and is sustainable. Your network should expand and develop as a result of your activities, and not shrink as you go about your task. It's a question of *How to Win Friends and Influence People* (Dale Carnegie,

1936) as opposed to *How to Lose Friends and Alienate People* (Toby Young, 2001). Making your network grow and sustain itself is about being professional, honest, clear and organised.

Networking takes time as well as effort. The contacts you make may not yield any results for weeks or months, if not years – alternatively you may meet someone who can help you immediately. While these might inspire you and get your attention, it's important not to neglect the seeds that you are sowing for the future. Remember John and Lisa.

WHAT'S YOUR STORY?

It's critical to have a rehearsed 'elevator pitch', or, as we call it at the Job Club, a 'Tell Me About Yourself' or TMAY. This is a short but engaging spoken introduction about you and what you have to offer. A good TMAY creates an interest or need in the other person. It should be between 30 seconds and two minutes in length and end with (if it's appropriate) a clear statement about what you are seeking. You'll be asked, 'What do you do?' hundreds of times, so there is no excuse for not having a solid response. Of course, it will be tailored to who is asking the question and to the context, but the principal points should remain simple and succinct. A TMAY is not an opportunity to give your life story. What people are really asking is: 'Tell me why I should talk to you now or see you again?' You have a few precious minutes to give them a good reason. What you did in 1986 or before is likely to be irrelevant. Keep it short; all you need is two or three sentences about what you can offer now with some evidence as to why you are believable.

PREPARING AND PRACTISING YOUR TELL ME ABOUT YOURSELF (TMAY)

Human beings are naturally curious about each other. A common way to begin a conversation is to ask: 'So, what do you do?' The social interaction often continues from there, yet how often have you asked someone else that question and been totally underwhelmed by the response? A poor response might be dismissive: 'Oh, this and that' or 'I get by, you know', which takes the conversation nowhere. The other extreme is to be overly detailed and therefore boring: 'Well, I am a chartered surveyor. I bet you didn't you know there are eight types of chartered surveyor. Let me tell you all about them. Firstly...' The fact is we all find it a simple question to ask, and we're all experts at judging the response. Listeners make up their minds very quickly about whether the speaker is worth listening to. Anecdotal evidence says an interviewer has made up their mind within two minutes of meeting you, and it could be even less at an open event with lots of other people in attendance.

When you are looking for work, you simply cannot afford to miss an opportunity. When someone says 'Tell me about yourself', you must be ready. That person is interested. They could offer you some excellent advice, be a potential employer or be able to refer you to someone useful. So how do you make an impact? The answer is: with preparation and practice. At each Job Club meeting, every attendee practises answering the TMAY question every week, and the other attendees are asked to give immediate feedback. Was it impactful? Did it show the speaker's strengths? Would you want to talk to this speaker again? When new members join the club, they're given written and spoken guidance on how to prepare for their first TMAY. Once a quarter, we invite a presentation-skills expert to help members improve.

These, then, are the Job Club's top seven tips on creating and improving your TMAY:

1. **Prepare it.** The average person speaks at around 125 words
   per minute. A two-minute TMAY is a 250-word mini-speech.
   You wouldn't give a speech without preparing in advance,
   and neither should you when there is a potential job at stake.
   Like a CV, it will never be perfect but the more you rehearse

and the more times you present it, the better it will be. You'll need to prepare a number of versions as every occasion will call for a slightly different response. Ideally, you should have three types: a formal version for use when you have one or two minutes of uninterrupted speaking time; a social version for informal gatherings when you want to amuse as well as engage and impress; and a one-line version for quick exchanges: 'I'm an author and an editor and I help people make books and get them published.'

2. **Have a structure.** As with any speech, your TMAY should have an impactful opening: something that grabs the listener's attention. Mention a little-known fact relevant to your profession, comment on a topical news item, or, if you can, amaze them with your job title: 'I'm the world's leading test pilot.' Your content must get your message across. Talk about relevant key facts and achievements from your work history that support the claim made in your opening line, and build towards a closing call-to-action. What is it you want from this person? Are you interested in meeting members of their network, obtaining advice, or exploring what the listener knows about your industry? This is the goal of your TMAY: including a call-to-action allows you to close powerfully. Here's an example of a structured TMAY: [Opening] *I'm an international tax advisory specialist with 15 years' experience in mergers and acquisitions at [company name].* [Content] *The projects I have worked on are... I managed teams in 23 countries and helped clients achieve tax savings of, typically... I have a reputation for...* [Close and call-to-action] *At the moment I'm looking to expand my portfolio of private clients and I wonder if you have any contacts at local companies with overseas subsidiaries looking to optimise their tax position.*

3. **Be factual and specific.** Talk about project budgets, sales revenues, numbers of people you managed, places you

worked in, industry specialities and qualifications you hold. If you are talking about employers, mention company names or give an indication of the size of the company if it is not a name the listener will recognise. Listeners like facts – it helps them answer the question in their mind about how you fit in to their view of the world.

4. *Keep it relevant.* The type of event, the background of the listener and the amount of time you have will determine which of your TMAY versions to use. At one end of the scale is the networking event where everyone has a two-minute slot to introduce themselves – this calls for a mini-speech with a structure as mentioned in No. 2 above. Alternatively, you might be asked your TMAY at a chance encounter or at a social event, where a one-line response is more appropriate. You must be the judge, and only practice will make you good at this.

5. *Practise, practise, practise (and get feedback).* Seek every opportunity to rehearse your TMAY. Try speaking it in front of a mirror, or recording it on video and playing it back to see what you look and sound like. Find events (like a Job Club meeting) where you can practise and get feedback in a safe environment. Finally, get out and use it. Every time you use your TMAY, it will get better – the more you speak, the more natural it becomes. Our view is that you should put as much effort into preparing and polishing your TMAY as you do for your CV. Then practise until you can deliver it with confidence to anyone, anywhere, at any time.

6. *Remember it's a mini-speech.* A TMAY is not a reading of your CV. Smile and make eye contact, use rhetoric and be passionate where appropriate. If you're talking about work you loved, inspiring people you have met, and successes that you are proud of, make sure your body movements and facial expressions match your words. Otherwise you aren't believable.

7. ***Engage the listener***. Are they showing signs of interest? Are they actively listening? If not, why not? Ask a question to check for comprehension. Adapt the content to their level of understanding. Remember you are aiming to stimulate interest. If a constructive conversation develops, or it engenders further questions, your TMAY is successful. When you introduce yourself effectively and in a professional manner, a whole new world of networking and contacts opens up to you.

DEALING WITH EMBARRASSMENT

When searching for a new role, many jobseekers are reluctant to contact people they know, especially after being made redundant. 'What do I say to someone who for the past five years I have been regaling with occasional news as to how well my career is progressing?' is a typical question raised at networking seminars. There is an assumption that, on hearing your news, the contact may assume, rightly or wrongly, that you have been made redundant for a reason that impacts your future capability to get a new job.

The truth, of course, is that there are all sorts of reasons why people are made redundant: reduction in staff numbers due to a decrease in incoming business, loss or termination of a major contract, poor business planning or closure of a department are a few examples. Whether or not your performance was adequate, compared to what the role demanded, is only one potential factor.

When assessing how to communicate with contacts after redundancy, consider the following: the reasons for your redundancy are for you to evaluate and act upon, and are not necessarily of interest to network contacts. Say, for example, you were in a sales position and were unable to make your targets for the year, and as a result you were asked to leave. It is in your personal interest to establish why you were not performing to the level expected – whether it was something that you could have changed, or whether the environment was simply not conducive to you giving your best. Whatever the reason, only you can take action to ensure it does not happen again.

When having that conversation with a network contact, the reasons why you were made redundant are best explained away factually and as efficiently as possible. 'I left ABC Ltd because they had a downturn in sales income and it was time to move on. I am now looking for...', or 'I left ABC Ltd when they closed the in-house printing department'. Focus on your skills, strengths, achievements, experience and what you are aiming to achieve now. Some contacts will assume the worst, but there is little you can do to change that. The majority will recognise that you have had a change forced upon you and you are taking positive steps to address it.

If you are still feeling awkward, reread the section on shame in Chapter 2. It is impossible to network effectively if you are ashamed of your situation. Resolve the issue before you go out and meet people.

MAKING CONTACT

When contacting others, it's important that you are clear and realistic about your goals. Whether by phone, e-mail, letter, online or in person, it's essential that you communicate exactly what you are seeking. People are more likely to help if it's within their capacity and they understand what you want. In a job-seeking context, you might be asking for:

- an introduction to someone else;
- advice on where to look for certain types of employment;
- a meeting to discuss a topic in more detail;
- a coffee to learn more about someone's role or how they achieved their position.

Research the person you are contacting. Determine their interests and hobbies; note if you have something to offer them, such as news about an old contact. That will make the conversation flow more easily.

If you are unsure about how to tackle a phone call, then script it first. The time you choose to make the call is totally up to you, so plan exactly what you will say and, if necessary, have the words written down in front of you.

MEETINGS

Eventually, networking by phone and e-mail will lead to face-to-face encounters. Treat each one as a business meeting and make sure you link the objectives you want to achieve to your networking goals. Respect the professional context – have some business cards prepared so that you leave people with something they can follow up. Despite the attempts of technology companies to encourage us to beam our details to each either from smartphones, the vast majority of networkers still exchange cards. And they need to be good-quality cards – not printed at home. A local printing shop or a specialist online business card supplier will do a great job for between £50 and £100 and provide you with something you're proud to leave with people. What to put on it? That depends on your goal, but in general make it as clear as possible what you do and how you can be contacted. If you're between jobs, a simple card stating your profession will do.

THE GOLDEN RULE: DON'T ASK FOR A JOB

Whether you are talking to old friends and business contacts, or meeting strangers at a networking event, there is one absolute rule: don't ask for a job. This is why you are networking, but getting straight to that question has one simple effect on the person you are talking to: it puts them on the defensive. The vast majority of people you meet (apart from recruiters and head-hunters of course) will not have a job for you. Even if they do have a job that might be suitable for you, how do they know you are the right candidate? Asking them straight out 'Do you have a job?' simply sets their mind thinking about how they will explain to you that they don't have one: what excuses to make up, what stories to tell. This is the opposite of what you want to happen. By talking about your interests and capabilities and, most importantly, what is going on for them in their world ('How's business?' or 'What projects are you working on?') you keep alive the possibility that (a) they may recall someone who you could talk to about putting your skills to use, and (b) they will remember your conversation and may well recommend you to someone in the future. Obviously, there is a remote chance they might have the job of your dreams ready for you and, in that event, the professional and businesslike way you have introduced yourself will only stand you in good stead in getting the role. However, it's best not to have expectations that this will happen.

NETWORKING EVENTS

As well as arranged meetings, part of your networking strategy may involve attending events where you have the opportunity to meet new people. Just as in a social context, the key here is to establish rapport before asking critical questions. The way to do this is to make it a two-way exchange of information. Then each person has a fair chance of assessing the other and arriving at an objective decision as to whether the potential relationship is worth pursuing.

The great thing about networking events is that you get to meet real people. No submitting CVs for approval or filling in application forms, it's an opportunity to meet other people who share your interests. The downside is that many of these people will not be directly useful. To maximise the chances of meeting suitable people, be selective in the events you attend. The 'right' event attracts people who will help you progress your networking or job-seeking goals. Examples include:

- industry trade exhibitions;
- chamber of commerce open meetings;
- networking meetings run by online groups such as ecademy;
- recruitment fairs;
- professional body events, e.g. Institute of Directors, Institute of Engineering and Technology, Chartered Institute of Marketing.

HOW TO WORK A ROOM

Meeting new people can be daunting for some. By following a few simple principles you can make it easier and more effective. Your objective is to meet people who might be useful to you. Some take a random approach: *I'll meet whoever will talk to me.* A more focused method is to scan the guest list, if provided, and decide who would be most useful to meet.

The first technique to master is the art of asking open questions. Open questions require an answer that contains some information about a person: their job, their company or their contacts. Eliciting this kind of response is by far the most efficient way of finding out about someone and whether or not they can be useful to you. The more you can find out about the person you are talking to, the more chance you have of discovering what might be of interest to them and whether they can help you in any way. To structure a conversation at a networking evening, it helps to follow a few simple rules.

1. Always ask permission to join in a conversation. *'May I join you?'* This always works to get you started, whether it is with one person or a group.
2. Ask questions about the past and the present to gain trust, build rapport and discover what this person might do for you, or you might do for them.
3. Ask questions about the future to establish whether there are any opportunities for you to help each other and develop the relationship. A typical conversation might begin :
   'Where have you come from?' or *'Have you come far today?'*
   'What does your company do?'
   'What is your role?'

Of course, you have to be prepared to answer the same questions with your own response – remember your TMAY.

At this point, you can evaluate how the conversation is going. Has it been really hard work? If so, swap business cards and make a polite exit, saying something like, *'It was nice chatting with you. If you don't mind I'm going to head off and get another drink.'* On the other hand, if it's going well, move the conversation further into the present: *'How do you do that? How is your business doing?'*

As the questions become more specific you begin to get a real sense of whether or not there is any common ground. A conversation might develop around some mutual interest, and if you feel there are some opportunities, this would be the time to develop the conversation around the future.

'Why did you come here tonight?'

Presumably they have a reason, like you do; perhaps it's because of something they want to happen in the future, such as more sales. This is your opportunity to think of ways to help the other person, by recommending a website, or some other information. If you have a means to prove your usefulness, even in a small way, you could be considered valuable to that person. Don't worry if you have nothing to suggest.

The final type of question begins with 'Who'. Since opportunities come to fruition in the future, use this part of the conversation to determine if the person is a useful contact. Remember, it's who you know and who they know that makes this a useful conversation for both parties.

'Who might you introduce me to?'

'Who should I be talking to about that?'

You can offer to introduce them to someone you know. You can also suggest a further meeting.

In summary:

- ask open questions: *Where? What? How? Why? Who?;*
- ask about the *past* and *present* and why they are there;
- ask about the *future* to discover how you can help each other.

BEING ORGANISED

It's critical to follow up as soon as possible with anyone you met who might be worth talking to again. Call or e-mail them, or set a time to meet. Send them the information or contacts you promised. Do what you said you would do – this is about being professional. Delivering on promises that you made is an important part of keeping your network growing. Whether you have volunteered information, contacts and/or introductions, make sure that you follow through. It's very dissatisfying to meet an interesting person at a networking event, agree there's something worth talking further about, exchange business cards and then never hear from them again. It takes very little energy to send an e-mail acknowledging you have met. The best networkers are assiduous in their follow-up. They go out of their way to ensure that each connection they make is followed through, and they do this because they are organised.

Without a system, networking can rapidly become hard work. When did you last see Gloria? What did she say? Who was it she introduced you to? And have you sent Chris that document and CV you promised him? Your system needs to allow you to track who you spoke to and when. It doesn't matter if you use a paper notebook, an Excel spreadsheet or Microsoft Outlook – whatever works for you.

The final and most vital part of your system is to take action on any job or work opportunities that arise. Remember that this is why you are networking; don't neglect to put time in your diary to relentlessly pursue every opportunity that has arisen out of your networking.

BUILD YOUR NETWORK

As you make and develop connections, more people will enter your network. It might be useful to have a method for categorising them so that you can decide how and when to continue meeting them. A category list for jobseekers might be:

6 - Not obviously useful

5 - I can help them in some way

4 - They can help me in some way

3 - They might have useful contacts

2 - They have influential contacts

1 - Bingo! They know of, or they are, someone who is recruiting.

This method could be added to your system so you know at any one time who your top-rated contacts are[1].

OTHER BENEFITS FROM YOUR NETWORK

Aside from work, jobs or contacts, there are many other advantages that you receive from your network. You will need other things in your job search or your working life that other people can provide. For example:

- honest and constructive feedback;
- positive suggestions and options;
- help to generate new ideas;
- mentoring from within their own effective support network;
- practical help, such as legal or IT;
- discussing your personal development;
- encouraging you to take action.

NETWORKING ONLINE

Employers today are more likely to turn to the Internet when researching any product or service, whereas only 10 or 15 years ago a guide such as the Yellow Pages would have been the first point of reference. Recruitment and job-hunting are no different, and now there are vast amounts of dedicated Internet resources to match jobseekers with potential employers.

Similarly, networking now has an online equivalent. Connecting with people online has opened up new opportunities that anyone seeking employment should exploit. With a little bit of effort, online facilities can play into the hands of the jobseeker, making their search more effective. For example, employers are likely to Google a prospective candidate at any level of seniority. The forward-planning networker will have put some effort into developing a professional Web profile. Equally, you can Google the person interviewing you and find out about their personal history, interests and previous employers.

Creating and maintaining an online presence is straightforward and it has many benefits. You can:

- make connections with specific people you want to meet;
- raise your profile by being active online, asking questions and providing answers for others;

- join local groups of online communities.

WARNING Being active online is not an excuse for avoiding people. It should be complementary to your meetings and telephone calls, and should not replace them completely.

CREATING AN ONLINE PROFILE

Mature jobseekers will relate to the fact that early on in our careers, having an online personal presence meant having your own home page. Some IT professionals had one, as did various celebrities or others obsessed with their own ego – or so we thought. In the 21st century all this has changed. It is now the norm to look for evidence of someone's capability or skills by doing a search online – try Googling the authors of this book, for example.

Why is this so? Primarily because technological advances have made it economically viable for others to provide the platform for us to do so at reduced cost. The plethora of networking websites allows the creation of an online profile at no cost (apart from your own time, of course) so you can instantly be visible to the global online community. In addition, having an online presence opens up a whole new world of networking – not only being found by people looking for someone like you, but connecting to people you want to meet.

The steps to creating an online profile vary according to which sites you use, but some general rules apply:

1. Be clear why you have an online profile. For example, is it to look for jobs or to showcase your skills to get consultancy work? If it's the former, then the format should be very similar to your CV, describing all you have done and when you did it. In the latter case, it's probably more effective to concentrate on those experiences that give you the credibility to be the skilled consultant you claim to be.
2. Choose a networking site that is most likely to yield the results you want. By far, the post popular networking site for

managers and professionals is LinkedIn. It's a great way to keep in touch with old colleagues, make contact with people in your industry, and find jobs and information. Don't overlook more socially-orientated sites such as Facebook and Twitter, which have a strong following in certain sectors, and where some jobseekers we've spoken to have been successful. Networking is partly about just keeping in touch and these sites enable you to do that efficiently and globally. Look for sites where the people you need to speak to are actively involved. Be aware that potential employers and clients can also access what you write online.

3. Register, using your real name and contact details. It's important that you look as professional online as you want to appear in person. This means not using nicknames, and having a genuine personal e-mail address.

4. Add as much detail to your profile as is relevant to achieving your objective. Look at other profiles to get ideas. Be as honest as you can, but be positive, especially if you are job-seeking.

5. Add a photo if you have one that's been professionally taken. Cropped holiday snaps, or a picture taken by a colleague in the office simply will not work. For a small outlay you can have a professional head-and-shoulders portrait done, which will stand you in good stead for the future.

6. Finally, look at your profile as an outside observer would see it or ask friends to offer an opinion. Unlike a paper document, changing it costs nothing, so don't be afraid to go back over the next few weeks, months and update it after others have commented.

MORE THAN AN ONLINE CV

Okay, so you have a profile on a networking website like LinkedIn. If you are someone with a fairly unique name, it won't be long before that profile has high visibility in Google rankings. Certainly anyone searching the networking site will find you. But this is more than an online CV, so what else can you do with it?

1. Connect to other people. Most networking sites allow you to make links to others online and build up a list of connections. It's a highly effective way of keeping in touch with ex-colleagues, or even current ones in a large organisation. The more people you can connect with, the larger your network, the greater the opportunity.
2. Search for people you want to meet. When you have found them online, find a way of connecting to them by asking someone in your network for an introduction.
3. Join and become active in professional interest groups, social groups or networking groups. Set up your own group on a particular topic and ask people to join. The more active you are, the more likely it is you will meet someone with the right opportunity for you.
4. Meet up. There is only so much you can accomplish through being virtually connected. Eventually, you must make e-mail contact, and then speak on the phone or make face-to-face contact. Sites such as ecademy, Refer-on and 4Networking encourage this by running a series of real meetings where people get together with others in a specific geographic area.

Don't forget the basics of online networking:

- have a photo professionally taken;
- use an e-mail address that is personal but still looks professional, for example: john.smith@gmail.com or mark@hotmail.com, rather than 2llivloc@freeserve.com (name unclear), or smithfamily@hotmail.com (unclear who will be receiving it);
- observe the rules of 'netiquette' of the group or online community;
- in order to boost your profile, regular small contributions are better than infrequent essays.

TIPS TO GET THE MOST OUT OF LINKEDIN

At the Job Club we run sessions specifically on how to optimise your use of LinkedIn. Having a profile as good as your CV is the first step. When that is done, what else can you do to promote your work search, whether you're looking for a job or clients?

1. Use the search function to find the active recruiters in a sector.
2. Join professional groups to converse with and meet new experts in your field
3. Search for jobs exclusively advertised on LinkedIn, and save those searches to get weekly alerts when a posted job meets your criteria.
4. Stay in touch with ex-colleagues.
5. Career changers – find people in your new career and ask them for advice.
6. Give and get recommendations, enhancing your profile and your credibility to employers and recruiters.
7. Research a company – do you know someone in your network who works there?
8. Ask questions/post answers in discussion groups to build your credibility on a topic.
9. Find a named contact in a company you are researching. Contact them, or even better, ask for an introduction from one of your contacts.
10. Research the work background and interests of your interviewer or client.

SUMMARY

Networking is the single most important skill that you can develop in order to get work. Like your career capital, it is something you will continue to build and develop throughout your working life. For any age group, statistics point to networking as being a more effective source in finding a job than any other method. For mature jobseekers it is often the only effective way to make progress. Your network is your most valuable asset.

LIAM'S NETWORKING STORY

Liam had 20 years' technical and management experience in the international telecommunications industry. As the father of two young children, he made a lifestyle decision to set himself up as an independent coach and consultant. He worked in career coaching and management training for several years, doing voluntary work with the Job Club and taking an associate role with a career management company. Recently, he made the transition back into mainstream corporate employment, and is now an executive at a renewable energies company. He made these transitions using his network.

When Liam left telecommunications, his network included hundreds of people in the field. He'd moved from job to job mainly on the basis of his reputation and contacts. He had some proven skills in key areas and he'd spent more time saying 'No' to new projects than looking for work. In his early 40s, it seemed a logical step to move on to being an independent consultant. He assumed it would only take a few calls and the work would come rolling in. How wrong he was.

His first obstacle was his lack of presence. Where he used to appear on organisation charts and distribution lists, be copied in on e-mails, meet useful people at random in offices, at airports or by coffee machines, now he was absent. As an independent consultant working from home or at a client's site, he had to make up for his lack of presence by being more active online, getting out and meeting people, and making contact by phone.

Liam learned that each network has its own culture. His corporate employment network had an unwritten rule: *This is a a network for people in full-time employment in the telecommunications industry*. As an independent consultant, although socially acceptable, professionally he was viewed very differently, even slightly negatively: *Aren't you just trying to sell to us?* was the unspoken question.

After three months of independence, Liam discovered that, although he had a very useful list of contacts, he didn't have the network he needed for new business. Where were the people to design a website, do accounts, coach and support, give legal advice, or just be there to discuss a new concept? A fresh network was required to support his new life as an independent consultant and executive coach. Two years later, his network included the following: a website designer; IT support; a brand consultant; an accountant and a legal adviser; a business and personal coach; three business partners; a new social group near to where he lives (rather than one based around work); people who gave him free, honest feedback on his business plans; companies that referred work to him; a public-speaking mentor; and, most importantly, clients.

For most purposes, if Liam wanted something done, needed a service or wanted to explore a new concept, the question he asked himself is not 'Where will I find someone who can help?' but 'Who in my network could help me with this?'

In the early days, he identified a number of networking groups that met locally and appeared to attract people like him. Attending on a monthly basis, he practised his TMAY and discovered what skills he could offer that were useful to others, in addition to developing beneficial contacts. Liam joined voluntary groups that could benefit from his advice and services. He met other like-minded volunteers, further developing his awareness of what made him different.

'Once you are out talking to people, new opportunities will present themselves,' Liam says. He once asked someone at a business networking function for advice on improving his public speaking skills and was introduced to Toastmasters, the public speaking education group. As it turned out, a local chapter met bi-monthly at a venue five minutes from his home office.

Joining local networking groups improved Liam's presentation skills and also proved useful in making more connections. Most importantly, he met and built relationships with people who became business partners. They completed several client projects together.

He volunteered to help run the local Job Club. The first 12 months were only about giving. He helped to set up the club and gave his time to run sessions; he researched and presented seminars on various topics. He also made contacts. He met an experienced careers adviser and, together, they went on to present paid-for workshops. Liam met others in his profession who provided him with advice and support, and the jobseekers he assisted eventually helped him by inviting him to participate in their opportunities and providing access to their contacts.

Networking became a key part of Liam's weekly business routine. *'Who is useful that I have met this week?'*, *'Who will I follow up next week?'* His networking became more targeted. *'Who do I know who knows someone who could be useful?'* A member of the Job Club spoke in glowing terms of a career management company. As this was a field that interested Liam, he asked for a professional introduction and his contact was only too pleased to do so. A few phone calls and meetings later, he was working as an associate for that organisation.

When the time came to focus on leaving the freelance sector and getting permanent employment again, Liam again turned to his network to find opportunities. He told a selective group of people that he was actively looking for a job, but without actually asking them for a job. It was the best way to ensure that his network was on the lookout for opportunities for him. This included networking with recruiters who were active in his sector. Six months after making the decision to return to corporate employment, Liam had two job offers on the table. The one he took came via an old university friend he happened to meet one day and who said casually: 'Oh, we're expanding, why don't you e-mail your CV?' Call it serendipity, but Liam makes the point that if he had not been actively networking in a focused way, he wouldn't have had the tools (a polished CV and a practised TMAY) and the presence of mind to take advantage of the opportunity.

UPGRADE YOUR SKILLS

Paul worked for a large corporation for over 15 years. During the recession of 2008/09, the company made huge reductions in staff and was on the brink of insolvency. As a result, Paul was made redundant. He found his skills as a technical product support manager were obsolete because his knowledge was restricted to the company's products. Paul recognised that his skills needed upgrading and he spent a portion of his redundancy package on technical training courses. He learned about other products and gained an industry-recognised qualification. This enabled him to apply for jobs in other technical support departments. His weakness, *'I only have skills with one company's products'*, had been turned into a strength: *'I am a qualified support manager with knowledge of a range of industry products and over 15 years' experience.'* He got a job within four months.

Paul's story is an example of a short, sharp fix. His skills upgrade solved an immediate problem and got him back in work again. Older workers need to continually update their knowledge to remain relevant and employable. Investing in your own development sends an important message to recruiters and employers: this person means business.

THE CRITICAL QUESTIONS

There are two primary reasons for an upgrade: either you need to develop your specialities and capabilities in your current career, or you have to learn something new to make a career or sector change. In the first case, it will be relatively simple to find out what you need. Ask yourself: 'What qualification/s do I need to get the job (or work) that I want?' For many, the answer will immediately spring to mind, as it did for Paul. If it doesn't, you'll need to do a bit of research. That will mean going online to discover which qualifications are a prerequisite for candidates in your field. Job adverts will tell you what you need to know, or you can speak with a recruitment agent. Another way to research involves using your network. This is an excellent time to get in touch with someone who is doing what you'd like to do. People generally like to talk about their work and if you can reciprocate by offering some help or taking them out for lunch, they will often be happy to tell you what's needed for your career. There is no substitute for first-hand information.

If you are changing careers you need to ask a second question: 'Who can tell me the best way to do this?' Again, first-hand information will help you to make the right decision about which course or institution is best. Seek out people who have made the transition you are considering. For example, if you've decided to become a teacher, find someone who's made the change and ask them how they succeeded. What training or educational route would they recommend?

Employers tend to value qualifications over experience. This is especially true when recruiters filter CVs before submitting them to an employer. For example, you may believe that your project management skills are well-developed or superior to others in your field, but most current job specifications for project managers state the candidate must have a PRINCE2 qualification, and you don't. The candidate with years of experience *and* the desired qualification stands a better chance of being put forward for interview.

The same thing is true if you have decided to be self-employed. A person who has chosen to go out as a consultant may find that their clients expect them to have a recognised qualification in their area of expertise. As an example, a certain type of project consultant will say their perceived value in the market is enhanced because they have a Six Sigma qualification on their CV. Some management consultants maintain that an MBA is essential.

If you've decided to run your own business – either by buying a pre-existing one, or creating a start-up business – you'll soon realise that, without training or relevant experience, your new business venture might fail. There are courses that can teach you how to start and manage a small business. In fact, courses are available for nearly every skill set or qualification that you can imagine.

A WORD OF CAUTION

Education providers are businesses and they need students in order to survive. They will be happy to take your money and offer no guarantee of employment after graduation. We refer to Professor Stephen McNair, an expert in adult education. With regard to career change in mid- to later life, he says he has not seen much evidence that a return to university will lead to an exciting new job. Take law for example. You may have decided that you'd like this career and you've found a university that will accept you, but will you be able to get a traineeship when you've completed your degree? You may find yourself competing with young graduates who are more appealing to law firms. Given that younger candidates are already getting jobs that you'd like to have, why put yourself in a similar position after years of retraining? As another example, coaching has become a popular choice for career-changers. Consequently, there are many providers who are happy to take your money and teach you how to become a business or life coach. The one thing that they can't promise – and that they often don't teach – is how to get work as a coach.

So there you have it: *caveat emptor* – let the buyer beware. We're saying that the best choice will be a course that will lead to employment. You're investing in yourself, and you'd like to see a return on your investment.

LEARNING FOR ITS OWN SAKE COULD LEAD TO A CAREER OPPORTUNITY

Studying a subject that you are passionate about is worthwhile, if you can afford the time and the tuition fees. There are no absolute rules in life. Pursuing your passion may lead to employment but, as McNair cautions, 'Don't assume it will make you rich.' Satisfying a long-term ambition may be a reward in itself; but consider anything else a bonus. Pippa's story illustrates how following a passion led to a new career.

SUCCESS STORY: **PIPPA**

A professional writer in her 50s, Pippa decided to return to university to get her MA in creative writing in order to pursue her dream of becoming a novelist. She had a valuable credit buried in her background, a bit of career capital that was lying there, waiting to be discovered and put to use. After she earned her new degree, she used her career capital to gain a part-time instructor position at her university. Pippa didn't set out to become a teacher; she discovered that it was possible only after she enrolled in the MA programme.

She began by researching UK universities and their entry requirements. As she imagined herself as a student, she realised she didn't want to travel far. She chose a local university that offered her chosen course, because she wanted to be near enough to attend events and activities without the added cost and time of commuting. It meant she was able to get involved. She joined clubs and organisations, volunteered to assist with special presentations, attended conferences and contributed to university publications. Pippa got noticed by the head of school, who recommended her to a contact who eventually offered her a job.

Pippa's career capital was valuable in a different faculty to the one where she was enrolled. After she became known in her faculty, she began to check out adjacent faculties and this is key to her story. Since she was taking a course that would teach her to write novels, she was perceived to be a novice in that area. But her screenwriting experience, and especially her 10-year-old credit for scripting a hit film, was valuable in the nearby film production faculty. They recognised her as an expert with professional experience in the world of work, a potential lecturer who would bring credibility and attract students to their faculty. Pippa was recommended by her module leader and her head of school. Through her volunteer work she'd proven herself to be a reliable and trustworthy person.

Before being offered a position, Pippa was asked to give a sample lecture. It was successful and she was offered a part-time position. The whole process took more than two years before she achieved a result.

Pippa's story shows that, aside from having talent and an obvious passion for your subject, there are some key questions you must answer: 'What have you achieved that is noteworthy?', 'What faculty would appreciate having someone with that achievement?' and 'Do you make the department more credible?' Universities need to attract students. That was their motive for hiring Pippa. She's now teaching part-time as part of a 'portfolio' (see Chapter 15) that allows her to combine a variety of creative jobs in a career that offers her the time to complete her novel.

SUMMARY

You can upgrade your qualifications with something very specific that will enhance your standing. Don't underestimate the value, especially to recruitment agents, of a qualification or accreditation on your CV, even though you have many years of experience.

You may be tempted to retrain for something completely new. We encourage you to think carefully and research your desired career path before you sign up for an educational programme.

Finally, if you pursue a private passion, be on the lookout for opportunities that may come your way. You never know where they might lead.

4

Move Forward: Get a Job

HOW TO FIND A JOB

Management and professional jobs are now advertised in ways that weren't previously possible. In the late 1980s, jobs were typically advertised via dedicated weekly sections in the national press or trade journals. Information about new jobs was concentrated with employers and recruitment companies or head-hunters. A professional wanting to change jobs in the mid-1990s might have used his or her contacts or made a couple of calls to head-hunters and agents to find out who was recruiting and, as a result, line up some interviews.

Today, information about job vacancies is accessible to everyone online. In March 2010, Google yielded 117 million results for the search term 'job site'. Faced with such a vast choice of websites, it can be difficult to know where to start or whether you should even bother to look for jobs online. It's never been easier to find and apply for any job you want, yet it is harder than ever to have your CV noticed and for recruiters to find the right candidate.

One effect of online job posting has been a rapid growth in the number of applicants for every position. By simplifying the application process 'Click here to apply NOW' and opening it up to anyone, recruiters and companies have removed the natural barriers to applying for a job. Potentially, billions of people can see every vacancy. To counter the huge number of applicants, many online postings have some fairly strict criteria: 'To apply for this job you MUST have the right to work in...', or qualifying questions such as 'To apply for this job you MUST be able to answer yes to the following...' Nevertheless, recruiters still report getting hundreds if not thousands of applications for each role advertised. Thus many jobseekers get disillusioned with searching and applying online and either neglect this as part of their job-hunting strategy or do it half-heartedly.

The task of making your application and CV stand out is more difficult than ever, but with some careful thought and planning, online job-hunting can be an effective part of your strategy. We'll explore all the job-search options and present techniques to help you online.

START WITH THE BASICS

It helps to understand how jobs are created. First, a company creates a need for more work to be done. For example, a sales force is taking on a new region, a new product launch requires additional marketing efforts, or a new business unit requires a managing director (MD). Alternatively, there may be a need to replace someone who's left the company. Either way, a job need has been created.

A member of staff will be assigned to deal with this need and, in a large corporation, a recruitment process is launched, which includes getting financial justification for hiring someone, having HR involvement to define the role, and so on. At the other end of the scale, a small business might decide that one person in the business, perhaps the MD, will take charge and find this new person. The search for likely candidates begins. This can involve everything from word of mouth, networking, employing recruitment agents or headhunters, or advertising online, in newspapers or in trade journals. There are three key stages at which a jobseeker can find out about a new role.

1. When a business is growing or changing and there is a need for additional or different work to be done, or a member of staff has left and needs to be replaced. No job has been advertised yet and the only way of finding out about the job opening is by using any contacts you have who are close to the business to discover that there may be an opportunity soon.
2. There is a defined need but the steps to advertise the role have not been completed. In this case, the person responsible for recruiting someone to fill the role may be open to direct approaches through a network.

3. The job is now advertised, either openly or via agents, and all interested applicants who are aware of the role can apply.

The first two stages are often referred to as 'the hidden job market' – that is, jobs that need to be filled but are not yet public knowledge. Stage three is when the majority of jobseekers enter the market for the job. This staged approach to filling roles is why it's often said that the majority of jobs are filled through networking. Stages one and two can take a long time – weeks, months or even years depending on how effective the company is at turning a defined need into action.

FILLING A ROLE – HOW IT WORKS

Here's an example of the process for filling a project manager role in a telecommunications company (with approximate timings).

Day 1: General acknowledgment of the need for additional resources on a project.

Days 2–30: Discussion between department heads and HR as to which departmental budget this new headcount would be allocated.

Day 31: Launch of internal financial approval process.

Days 32– 40: Creation of the detailed job specification by the manager, including research into the appropriate salary range.

Days 40–60: Case to hire goes through approval process by Finance, HR and department managers.

Day 61: Job posted internally for a minimum of six weeks.

Day 100: Job posted externally to agencies.

In the example above, more than three months elapsed from the day that the need for recruitment was acknowledged until the role was advertised externally. During that time, the manager was open to receiving recommendations of suitable candidates to fill the role from his network of contacts. By the time official approval

> was given and the role posted, a shortlist of potential candidates already existed. Any candidate who had access to information about the job when it was 'hidden' had a much greater chance of success than someone who applied during the formal process.

An effective job-hunting strategy addresses the hidden job market and the advertised jobs market in equal measure. 'Hidden' jobs are much harder to track down, but once you have found one, your chances of success are much higher. Competition is reduced as the role has not yet been advertised, and the hiring manager and the company can save time and money by selecting a good candidate without incurring the cost of advertising or agents' fees. Depending on how you heard about the job, your name and reputation might already be known to the company or hiring manager.

ACCESSING THE HIDDEN JOBS MARKET

Essentially there are two ways of doing this. The first is by networking – who do you know, who do they know, and how can you engage with them to learn about what's going on and where? A second approach is to identify companies that you think you *might* want to work for, contact them directly and hope that your enquiry lands on the desk of someone who is looking to hire.

The networking techniques we described in Chapter 7 are invaluable when it comes to identifying hidden jobs. Building your contact list is a long-term game and sometimes it's hard to see where the results will come from. However, getting out there and talking to your contacts is the best way of ensuring that if someone in your network hears of an opportunity you'll find out about it. A key point to note here is that the people in your contacts' networks will often be more useful to you than your own contacts, because yours will likely move in the same circles as you. Second-degree connections might operate in completely different circles, so you can really expand your range of opportunities by using them. Let your network know you're available and ask for recommendations or suggestions for new contacts.

Networking works both ways. The managers responsible for hiring are also networking to find people. They will ask their contacts if they know someone – maybe you – who can fill the role.

When networking, don't overlook the obvious. A recent visitor to the Job Club was a foreign national who had the right to work in the UK. After attending the Job Club session on networking, he identified that one of his most obvious and unexploited networking opportunities was to approach people of his own nationality working in the UK. He already knew many of them. Sure enough, after working that part of his network, he landed the job he was seeking.

With a direct approach, you identify companies who require people with your skills and then target them with an e-mail or a letter campaign. The challenge is to identify which companies to approach. There are over 2 million registered companies in the UK and you can use the Companies House database, available online. Here's a list of criteria for filtering them:

- location – within X miles from your home;
- industry sector, or activity description;
- size (by number of employees or turnover);
- age (e.g. companies less than three years old);
- ownership (are they a subsidiary of an multinational?);
- export revenue (do they do business internationally?).

Compile a list of addresses and directors' names; then draft a letter. Although an e-mail is simple, quick and inexpensive, it may not be possible to obtain the e-mail address of the person you want to contact, and even if you do, your e-mail may get lost in their inbox. A paper letter, on the other hand, stands out. It takes more time and effort and it costs more, but will almost certainly have more impact. Here are some key points:

- Remember the old-fashioned rules of letter-writing. Use high-quality paper and print it on a good printer or use a print shop;
- Think carefully about what to put in the letter. It should have a compelling message, rather than being a long list of things that you are good at. It's far better to make a bold and assertive claim to be really good at one or two things. The point is to get the readers' attention, which could lead to them reading your CV and/or having a meeting with you;
- Write the greeting, salutation and the address on the envelope by hand. This makes your letter stand out.

A letter targeted at an industry sector will have a response rate similar to direct marketing campaigns, which is somewhere between one and eight per cent. It will require hundreds of letters to have a reasonable chance of success. Your hit rate may be higher if you have a specific skill and you know the range of companies that need people with this skill. You may want to send all your letters in one batch or plan to send them over a period of time, say 50 per week over a period of two months.

Like any direct marketing campaign, you'll need to set up a system for tracking the progress of your letters. Who have you sent them to, who has responded, which ones are worth a follow-up phone call?

A successful letter campaign will result in a number of networking and job opportunities. Some of these will be informal (*Come in for a chat*), while others may be more formal (*We have an interview day in five weeks' time. Please apply via our website and I'll ensure you get selected*). These responses then need to be followed up as described in the next chapter.

Table 9.1 opposite summarises the different approaches to accessing 'hidden' jobs.

	Pros	Cons	Tips
Networking and personal introduction	The person you are introduced to already has a level of trust in you because of the recommendation.	Each case has to be managed on its own merits. May be a long-term game.	Use your network extensively. The people your contacts know are probably more important than your direct contacts as they have access to a different range of companies and contacts.
Direct approach	Identifies many jobs in the hidden job market that are outside your network.	Costs of sending a letter or e-mail to potentially 100s of companies. Response rates can be very low typically <8%.	Develop a target list of companies based on specific criteria. Write a compelling letter stating what you offer and how it could provide benefit to the company. If possible, follow up with a phone call.

Table 9.1

FINDING ADVERTISED JOBS

Despite statistics claiming that many jobs are filled through networking and direct approaches, it would be foolish to ignore the advertised jobs market. In fact, in the public sector there is legal obligation to advertise new or vacant posts and it will be necessary for you to apply via a standard process.

Table 9.2 lists the main sources for finding job advertisements. Where you look will depend on the type of work you're seeking and your industry or profession. Some professionals find that an online version of their trade journal is by far the best source. On the other hand, if you are looking for a career change, you will find general job boards immensely useful because they allow searches for a variety of different roles. Equally, professions that require specific qualifications, such as PRINCE2 or PMI certification, lend themselves to online job board advertising because jobseekers can do a search using these keywords. Those looking for a general management position will need to use a more specific search term than 'manager'.

	Pros	Cons	Tips
Jobs or careers pages on company websites	Can be very informative about careers at a company. Lists open positions and role details.	Single company only; need to check regularly for updates.	Use e-mail alerts if available, or diarise a time to check the sites regularly.
Company websites that invite speculative CVs	Indicates openness to speculative applications. May give general info about type of candidate sought.	You never know if there are any vacancies. Your CV might disappear into a black hole.	Always follow up with a phone call. If it's a general number, ask for the HR Manager.
Job boards such as monster.com, jobserve.com, executive-appointments.com (including sector-specific job boards)	Thousands of jobs in multiple sectors and locations.	Requires careful use of search terms to identify jobs to apply for. Impossible to tell whether jobs advertised are 'real' or posted by individuals and/or organisations fishing for CVs.	Spend time learning which search criteria yield the type of job you are looking for. Sign up to 'jobs-by-email' services on boards which have the sorts of jobs you are looking for.
Networking sites e.g. Linkedin.com	Mainly managerial and professional roles; often used by companies and individuals to recruit directly. Allows you to research company contacts.	As with job boards, roles might not be authentic, and will require careful use of search terms.	Maintain an up-to-date online profile that summarises your key skills. Obtain recommendations from trusted colleagues.
Recruitment agencies and consultants	Will work hard on your behalf to get you into a role, IF you are a good candidate. Might be the only route a company is using to recruit.	Can become very demoralising if agents don't reply to your calls or emails. This is normally because they are flooded with applications for a role.	Spend time discovering which agents have the most jobs in your sector, then cultivate relationships with named people at those agencies.

Table 9.2

	Pros	Cons	Tips
Head-hunters	Have a defined brief for a specific person. If you are a good match you will be in demand.	Not interested in assisting you if you do not fit any of their current roles.	When in work, be open and helpful to head-hunters who call you. You never know when you might need them!
Newspaper adverts, including local newspapers	Limited number of jobs presented so it's easy to check. Probably targeting a specific sector each day ('London jobs', 'public sector jobs' etc.).	Limited number of jobs advertised. Many companies and agencies using online advertising only.	Use in addition to other job-seeking techniques, not as your only method.
Trade journals	Very useful for specialists looking for roles in a specific sector e.g. construction, education, nursing. May have an online equivalent.	Tend to be roles for people with experience in that industry; not good for career changers.	Identify those publications relevant to you and ensure a regular scan is part of your job-seeking routine.
Aggregating job sites and boards e.g. Indeed.com	Offer a service where jobs from many sources, including other job boards, are aggregated and search-enabled.	Number of jobs available very high so search criteria have to be fairly specific.	Find those which include the sorts of jobs you are looking for and sign up for e-mail alerts.

Table 9.2 cont'd

To avoid searching job boards manually on a daily basis, use keywords to set up e-mail alerts from job sites. This will ensure that roles matching your criteria are sent to you as soon as they are posted. The more advanced search facilities have filters that allow you to define your search criteria, based on salary offered, location (or even distance from your home) and other objective parameters. Your principle objective when setting up alerts is to be notified of as many suitable jobs as possible.

Ask yourself: 'What specific terms will be used to describe the role I am looking for?' Often the job title alone is not enough. For example, searching for a project director or sales director position will yield many jobs, but will they be in the right industry? You will need to use additional qualifying terms to narrow your search. If you were searching for a sales director position for a specialised software product, it would be more useful to do a search on both the software name and a salary level. Find a job board that has appropriate jobs and experiment with different search terms until you arrive at ones that yield the results you expect. Note that the more specific the search terms, the fewer results you will see. That's not a bad thing as it may reflect the reality that the type of jobs you are seeking are few and far between. In that case, patience may be required while you wait for your e-mail alerts to inform you of any suitable posts. If you have very specific criteria, you may need to adopt a different job-search strategy.

SHOULD YOU PAY FOR ACCESS TO JOB BOARDS OR TO THE HIDDEN JOBS MARKET?

In principle, no. If employers want you to apply for roles, it is in their interest to make them as widely available as possible. Some job boards (**theladders.co.uk** and **ivyexec.com** are two examples) now request a membership fee in order to view and apply for certain executive jobs. In the case of **theladders.co.co.uk** there is an opt-out button, but some jobseekers have reported difficulty finding it. A few career management companies also offer access to the hidden jobs market in exchange for a fee. You do get something for your fee: an enhanced service level and bespoke search capability, or access to personal career advice. It's up to you to decide whether these are worth paying for. But paying simply to access a list of vacancies and for the privilege of applying is not something we would recommend.

HEAD-HUNTERS AND RECRUITMENT CONSULTANTS

Acting as agents between the jobseeker and the employer, head-hunters and recruitment consultants are often much maligned. In our experience this stems from a misunderstanding of the roles these people play, so let's look at what they do.

Head-hunters are paid by an employer to search for candidates for a specific role. The role is probably not advertised and the head-hunter has a detailed specification. They will trawl through their contacts: past clients, referrals, CV databases and LinkedIn, to identify a shortlist of recommended candidates. The head-hunter is paid by the employer and usually receives a percentage of the role's salary. If you know the names of head-hunters operating in your sector, it's worth sending them your CV so they can add your name to their database. Don't expect them to do any work on your behalf unless their client, the employer, has a role for which you might be suitable. Be prepared to be ignored.

Recruitment consultants, or agents, also have the employer as their client, but typically work to fill defined roles which are openly advertised online. They may recruit roles for many different companies at any one time. Having identified suitable candidates, the recruitment agent will select a few names to put forward to the employer and then work with jobseekers and employers to set up interviews. Recruitment consultants are paid by the employer, usually a percentage of the role's salary. Some recruitment agents work on a retainer, i.e. the employer pays them a regular fee to conduct ongoing searches and selections on their behalf. In this instance, the employer has chosen one recruitment agent to manage all their recruitment, as opposed to using different agents on a contingency basis.

To find suitable recruitment agents, search the job boards to identify which agents are active in your sector. If you apply for an advertised role, use this as an opportunity to establish a relationship with the agent who is most active in your sector. Contact your network of jobseekers to learn which agencies are useful. There are thousands of agents and it is critical that you establish good relationships with a selected few (more than one, but fewer than ten) and stay in contact on a regular basis. Don't waste time with agencies that clearly don't offer suitable roles.

RECRUITMENT AGENCIES: PROBLEMS AND SOLUTIONS

Our personal experience is that there are some excellent recruitment agents out there and we respect the industry as a whole. So why do agents get such bad press from older jobseekers? It's often because candidates' expectations are high or they haven't found the right ones to work with. But there is another reason: some recruitment agents use questionable practices. Here are a few examples:

1. Job advertisements that aren't real jobs

This practice is called 'CV farming'. Some agents do this in order to add to their databases. Be wary if the job is not well specified or vague, or if the salary seems too high. If it sounds too good to be true, it probably is.

2. Cowboys and time-wasters

There are no bars to entry to the recruitment profession, so check your agent's credentials. Do any of your industry colleagues know of the agency? Is the individual on LinkedIn? Have they got recommendations? Are you dealing with a junior member of staff? What knowledge do they have of your industry sector?

3. Calls or interviews just to meet targets or key performance indicators (KPIs)

Agents have targets for the number of telephone calls they have to make, and the number of new clients to see each week. Be wary of the promising call that arrives out of the blue, or the initial interview that they suddenly want to have with you. You might be just another tick in the box for an agent trying to meet targets, and there is no real opportunity. The only way to get around this is to focus your energies on developing a relationship with a few agents that you can trust.

Recruitment agents can do you a great service: the key is finding one who recognises your value and will work on your behalf. How do you do it? Here are three suggestions:

1. Choose carefully

Spend time researching which recruiters in your chosen field are actually getting results. Use your contacts in the industry to find out which agents are effective.

2. Be memorable

Have a CV that shows your specialities clearly: what you're *really* good at, so that the recruiter can see your obvious marketable value. Recruitment agents don't like 'jack of all trades' CVs: they're impossible to sell. When speaking to an agent for the first time, use a rehearsed script (a special TMAY for the purpose, as described in Chapter 7).

3. Demonstrate enthusiasm

If you see a suitable role, show keenness and tenacity. Chase for updates; respond promptly to e-mails and messages. *How* you apply for jobs says a lot about what sort of person you are.

'WHY DO RECRUITMENT AGENTS NEVER CONTACT ME?'

Imagine a postman doing his rounds. For every address for which there is no post that day, he knocks on the door and says: 'I'm really sorry, but there's no mail for you today. But keep your hopes up. There might be some tomorrow. I'll let you know'. He's very popular with people on his route – they love being kept up to date. But his manager is furious. Why is his delivery rate the lowest in the district? Unlike that postman, an agent won't contact you if there is no message.

If you find that recruiters aren't returning your calls and e-mails and this goes on for weeks and months, STOP. It's not working. Try a different approach. Change your CV. Apply for different jobs. Contact different recruitment agents.

A final point: recruitment agents are young and ambitious and most of them want to be head hunters. That's where the money is. It's no wonder that they will not waste time on a candidate who they believe will be unsuccessful, or who doesn't instantly fit a profile.

SUMMARY

There are many methods of searching for job vacancies and the most suitable ones for you will depend on the type of job you're looking for and your level of seniority. A combination of methods is likely to work best initially, in order to flush out where the relevant jobs are advertised. Then you can focus on the methods that yield the most rewards. With so much information online, good research followed by focus and perseverance gets the best results.

Networking and speculative approaches statistically produce the most successful results for the mature worker. However, these methods take time. In the short term, they may appear to offer scant return for your effort, but they usually pay off in the end.

SUCCESS STORY: **ANNE BURCHETT**

A break from employment might be necessary for any number of reasons, and frustration with your current situation can be one of them. At the age of 46, Anne Burchett took a carefully planned leave in the form of a voluntary redundancy – with a plausible reason for taking time out – but getting back into work was more difficult than she anticipated. Her advice to anyone who needs a break is worth heeding.

Born and educated in France, Anne started work in 1985 after leaving business school. She soon landed a role in an industry she is still passionate about: the wine trade. Anne was UK and Germany Export Manager for Chantovent, a position that gave her the opportunity to move to England in 1989. She left when part of the company was sold, and her next role was UK Sales and Marketing Director for Skalli, a company selling varietal wines from the south of France. Later she was head-hunted by Waverley as Off Trade Sales and Marketing Director. Anne worked there until 2000, when she was made redundant as the result of a corporate sale. She worked on several consultancy projects: one of them was with Vinival, a Loire wines company, and it led to her appointment as UK Sales and Marketing Director. She stayed on in a slightly altered position when the company was sold in July 2004 but was made redundant nine months later.

With her reputation firmly established in the industry, it was only two months before Anne was approached by Castel and offered the position of UK Managing Director. The next three years were challenging and Anne decided to take a year off to take stock. She negotiated a voluntary redundancy with her employer and announced that she was leaving to study for an MA in creative writing.

After she received her new degree in 2009, she felt ready to return to business. But it was a bad time for employment everywhere, and for the wine trade in particular. And yet she was able to get a job six months after graduation. How did Anne do it? She kept her network alive during her break. She attended wine tastings and talked to people. She stayed in contact with friends and associates, always reminding them that her absence was temporary. To keep her hand in, she worked on small consultancy projects while studying for her MA. She updated her personal information and CV on LinkedIn, using it to keep in touch with her colleagues and making it possible for employers to check her out at a distance. By doing those things, Anne was visible while she was away.

Success was not achieved by using agencies or answering advertisements. It came about through her personal contacts. Sopexa, a private agency for PR and promotion (specialising in food and wine) offered her a job as UK Managing Director because they were aware of her availability and they'd already assessed her work through one of the consultancy projects she'd worked on. After passing a rigorous series of interviews and tests she got the job. (Note that she stayed in the industry but changed from selling bottles to promoting them.)

She has some good advice for those seeking re-entry after a break.

- Be prepared to justify your temporary leave. It must be perceived to be for a good reason. 'Time off with the children' or 'I need a break' is not acceptable in a competitive market.
- It's easier to stay within your industry where you have a reputation, contacts and relevant experience.
- Use the people you know – they're your best resource.
- Resist the temptation to take rejection personally.
- Be patient.
- While in work, spend your time building contacts that may be useful in the future – you never know when you might need them.

HOW TO APPLY FOR A JOB

This chapter is divided into two parts. First we deal with the application process in general, then we tell you what you need to know to create one of the most essential tools for the jobseeker: the curriculum vitae, or CV.

PART 1: THE APPLICATION

A manager with a vacancy to fill has a simple objective: to find the best available person they can afford for the role. They may have a choice of just one applicant, or thousands. Your objective is to be one of those people, ideally the only one, whose application is attractive enough to warrant an interview, not only in terms of content and presentation, but also *how* it arrived on the recruiter's desk.

The process of applying for a job is an important step. What you put in your application determines whether or not you get to the next stage. The way you manage your application sends an important message to the recruiter about your work habits, and will therefore influence the selection process.

As a mature worker, you face three challenges:

1. Being organised in your search, perhaps after years of steady employment.
2. Condensing decades of skills and experience into a short CV.
3. Overcoming resistance from employers and recruiters to employing someone who is, on paper, overqualified.

We will address these issues in the context of two scenarios:

1. Applying for a job that you know is available through a personal recommendation, a network contact or as a result of a speculative approach;
2. Responding to a job advertisement. The job might be advertised directly by the employer, or it could be advertised on their behalf via an agent. Either way there will be rules to follow in order to be considered.

Getting organised

If you've been in long-term employment, it's possible that you have not had to put together a job application for some years, so take time to set up the resources you need. The essential tools you must have before applying are as follows.

1. A desktop or laptop with Internet access, or reliable access to one. Even if you send a paper CV and letter, the vast majority of applications will involve electronic communication and online research.
2. A 'professional' e-mail address, for example: name.surname@gmail.com. The name should match the name on your CV and should not sound flippant. For example: name@hotmail.com or name56@tesco.com are acceptable, but chelseano1@anyoldisp.com, dancinglady@myhotmail.com are definitely out. They don't match the name on your CV and they certainly do not convey the image of maturity and professionalism that one would expect from an older worker. It will stand you in good stead to create a professional-sounding e-mail address for your job applications.
3. A telephone number that will be answered appropriately. It's acceptable in most business cultures to use your mobile number on applications, instead of your home telephone number. If you do give your home number, inform anyone who is likely to answer the phone that you might receive a call regarding a new job. If using your mobile, then make sure the voice-mail message is appropriate for someone seeking employment.

4. A CV, bio, career summary, resumé, employment history – whatever the name, you will need a document that accurately reflects who you are and what you are offering for the position. Later in the chapter we will cover the principles of preparing an appropriate CV for the older worker.

5. A system for recording what you have sent and when – you can buy this or set up your own spreadsheet. If you are likely to be applying for just one or two jobs per month, the system can be in your head, but if you are planning to apply for five to ten jobs per week you'll need a paper or computer-based logging system. Bear in mind the call from a recruiter regarding your interest in a role can come at any time. Your system should allow you to quickly access:

- the job advertisement, and where you saw it;
- a copy of the CV that you sent;
- a record of any previous conversations about the role.

Whether it is a paper-based filing system, one totally based on your powers of recall or a Microsoft Outlook contact management system with a supporting CV database, work out something that is appropriate for you.

MAKING APPLICATIONS

How you submit your application will depend on whether it is a company you are approaching directly or whether you are replying to a job advertisement.

The direct approach

You have identified a job for which you are qualified, or a company that interests you. This could be through a personal recommendation, a network contact or the outcome of a company search, as explained in the previous chapter. These are informal applications where there are no set rules to follow.

If you're submitting your application to someone you know, then what you have done so far has been positive in that it has got you noticed. The next steps will very much depend on the exact circumstances. Your application could consist of a letter or e-mail summarising why you are interested and asking about the next steps. It might not be a good idea to send a CV until you know more about the potential role. If someone has formed a mental image of your capabilities based on a third person's recommendations, it would be foolish to undermine this by sending a CV that demonstrates that you have few qualifications in the sector. The purpose of a CV is to open the door to a conversation or interview, so if you are already at that stage, it may be irrelevant. If a CV is requested, the best course of action is to research the position so you can send a CV that is tailored to the role.

If you're making a speculative approach, you'll be using your list of companies and contact details that you created in the previous chapter. Your letter should state why you are writing, what you can offer, and conclude with a request for further communication. A recommended structure is to open with a compelling statement about yourself, or something topical relating to the industry and why this has made you interested in the company. The body of the letter should state clearly three or four benefits you could bring to the company if they were to employ you. Refer back to the self-assessment you completed in Chapter 4 for a list of your responsibilities and achievements. Select those of greatest relevance to the company you are approaching so that you can sell yourself in terms of the benefits you can offer to the employer. The final paragraph should cover what you expect the next step to be. Will you be calling to enquire whether your letter is of interest? If so, when?

Attached to the letter should be a CV, ideally a single-page summary CV. This adds credibility to your letter. Remember you are not applying for a job here but trying to stimulate interest in yourself so that someone from the company will want to meet you to discuss potential roles. They may call to request a more detailed CV, if required.

Responding to a job advertisement

This requires more detailed preparation as you will already have greater knowledge about what the recruiter is looking for. Whether the advertisement was posted online, on a company website or in a national newspaper or a trade journal, a well-written job advertisement lists every requirement you need to know to make a good application. A good job advertisement will describe:

- the company or department and working style or culture;
- the title, location and responsibilities of the role, and, possibly, salary and benefits;
- the essential and desirable skills and experience;
- how to apply and when – the rules.

Sometimes it will be necessary to read the job advertisement a number of times and interpret what is written in order to establish the exact requirements. At other times the requirements will be explicitly listed. It may be possible, on enquiring, to obtain a more detailed job description for the role.

The first step in the application process is to decide whether there is a good fit between you and the role. There are two questions to ask yourself:

1. How many of the essential and desirable skills and experience criteria do I meet?
2. What do I know about the working style of this organisation and how likely am I to fit in?

Deciding if you're likely to fit in with the working culture is often difficult to gauge from a job advertisement or job description. As a mature jobseeker you probably know enough about the working styles and cultures that suit you. Refer to your self-assessment as a reminder. As you go through each job application process, try and gather as much information as possible from the recruiter (and the interviewer, when the time comes) to determine whether or not you will fit.

The skills question lends itself to a more objective analysis. The 'essential' and 'desirable' skills of the desired candidate are clearly specified. How does your skill set measure up against them? Be as honest as possible.

- *Essential* implies that these are requirements which if not met will exclude you from the application process.
- *Desirable* are those skills or experience that an employer will use to further assess the applicants once all the essentials are met.

In a very competitive job market it may be that most candidates will have all the essential skills and some, if not all, of the desirables. The bar has been raised. How do you decide if it is worth applying? The harsh truth is that you will soon discover this for yourself by the responses you get to your early applications. Seek out feedback from agents and recruiters. Factor the answers into your decision-making for later job advertisements.

Once you have established that it is worth applying, you can move on to the next stage and compose your application.

The key steps are:

1. Reread the advertisement until you are crystal clear about what the employer seeks. Note any instructions as to how to apply.
2. Compose a covering e-mail or letter, and a CV, all of which should be tailored to the role. Describe yourself positively and match your skills to the requirements.
3. Submit your application in the required format by the closing date.

It is imperative that you follow any application instructions, especially if the recruiter has specified the use of an application form. The application form makes the recruiters' job easier, because all the applicants are forced to present their information in the same way. If an application form is specified, it's not acceptable to send a CV. Doing so is the easiest way to disqualify yourself from consideration.

MAKING YOUR APPLICATION RELEVANT

A typical problem for the mature jobseeker is that you will very often have a broader range of experience and skills than is required for the job. Sending a full work history will potentially rule you out because you will come across as having plenty of general skills but nothing specific to the role, or you will give the impression of having done it all before, leaving the employer wondering why you want the role.

When preparing an application, ask yourself: 'What are the top three to five attributes that I think the employer is looking for?' If it is an advertised role, these attributes will be listed. If not, some research among your network might be required. Focus on these attributes when selecting what to include from your repertoire of skills and experience. Make a table. In one column list the criteria the employer is looking for, and in the other your achievements, qualifications and experience – the things that demonstrate you have the skills and you meet the criteria.

Your application should be a complete chronological record, but what you say about each job and the skills and competencies you describe should be limited to those that are relevant. You are not trying to illustrate *all* the things that you are good at, but trying to show that you are *really* good at the specific skills required for the role you are applying for.

The top three to five reasons that make you suitable for the role should then appear:

- in your covering letter or e-mail;
- in the top third of your CV, usually in a 'profile' section;
- in any accompanying or supporting information.

The body of your CV should now back up the claims you make in the covering letter and profile. In your employment history, list the responsibilities and achievements that verify the statements you have made. Likewise, only add the educational and qualification information that is relevant.

When you read through your application for the job, it should be obvious that you have picked from your extensive background and experience only those elements that qualify you to do the job. Your capability should be evident. If it's not obvious to you, how do you expect a recruiter to spot it in 30 seconds? Typically, that is how long your application has to make an impression.

IMPORTANCE OF FOLLOWING UP

An employer or recruitment agent wants to know that job applicants are interested in the role on offer. All else being equal, the applicant who follows up with a phone call or e-mail a short time after sending their application, will stand out over those who just send it in and hope. Don't harass the employer or agent with calls, but do make sure that they know you are interested in the outcome of your applications. Is it 'yes', 'no' or 'we'll keep you on file'? And if it is 'no', is there any feedback on 'why'?

Many recruitment agencies and companies now openly declare: 'If you don't hear from us, assume that you were not successful.' This is in response to criticism from jobseekers that they never hear anything back. Even if this is the case, we would argue that if you are a good candidate for a role, it is always worth trying to get through by phone to demonstrate your real interest.

DEALING WITH REJECTION

Recruitment is a selection process. You are being assessed along with other candidates, who, like you, think they are suitable for the role. When rejections come in you have to see them as a natural part of the process, just as in a marathon race where there is one winner and many participants. The selection process is dependent on attracting many applicants, all of whom will be rejected except one. Rejection does not invalidate the skills and experience you have to offer.

It is important, however, to act on trends in the feedback you receive. Is there a common theme? Are you applying for the right roles? Does your CV need a makeover? Review the reasons for rejection, accept that it does not invalidate who you are, and then change your approach if you think it's appropriate.

MOVING FROM PUBLIC SECTOR TO PRIVATE SECTOR EMPLOYMENT

At a 'Beat the Credit Crunch' seminar in June 2009, the solution proposed for jobseekers was to seek government and public sector contracts – at the time their funding appeared unlimited and guaranteed. The public sector accounted for 20.9 per cent of UK employment[1]. Many roles were filled by ex-private sector employees.

The change was radical. In October 2010, the government announced that almost 500,000 public sector jobs would be lost in the next five years. Companies and consultancies serving the public sector were forced to radically scale back their business expectations. In 2011 and beyond, the pendulum will swing and ex-public sector workers will be seeking employment in the private sector. If you're one of them, how will you face the challenge?

WHAT'S THE DIFFERENCE BETWEEN THE TWO SECTORS?

By public sector we mean all jobs that are funded directly or indirectly by central, regional or local government. These include the NHS and the armed forces. By private sector, we mean the employer is a privately-owned company seeking to maximise profit for shareholders. Many jobs perceived to be in the public sector have already been outsourced to the private sector and so the lines are blurred. Some private companies provide services exclusively to, or on behalf of, the public sector. Service companies like Serco, Connaught, Siemens and Accenture provide services to government under long-term contracts.

Some private sector employers have a perception that employees in the public sector work in a sheltered environment and are therefore less professional. In fact, public sector employees are often equally committed and professional, but it's a different type of professionalism. To find employment, you'll need to challenge the stereotypes. Furthermore, you'll need to demonstrate how skills developed in the public sector can be applied in the private sector.

As an example, we recently learned that a small private company, a start-up specialising in the global export of IT equipment, had a recruitment problem. The ability to travel widely at short notice to developing countries, and work in small teams to manage complex local relationships were key requirements of the role. It proved difficult to find candidates in the private sector – but two public sector groups were sources of candidates: ex-UK Foreign Office and ex-UK armed forces personnel with engineering or signals expertise. These people have a well-developed ability to operate on their own initiative far from home – a highly-valued skill for this private company.

APPLYING FOR JOBS IN THE PRIVATE SECTOR

Research the opportunities where your transferable skills will be valued and use the tools and techniques described in this book. The table below identifies some of the specific differences to note when making the change from public sector to private sector, and how to tackle them.

APPLYING FOR JOBS IN SERVICE COMPANIES

The new environment is one that is highly scrutinised. Service companies may be private operations, but they are spending from the public purse. You'll need to demonstrate you can work to targets, operate in a fast-moving environment, and be able to change direction and bring stakeholders with you. Employers

Public sector	Private sector
Job titles will include terms such as 'officer' and may be strictly graded based on seniority.	Job titles tend to be made up as required. It's important that you investigate what your 'public sector' title would correspond to in the industry or company you are applying to. Use this terminology on your CV.
Typically direct recruitment via a website, newspaper adverts and internal HR department. Speculative applications will be discouraged.	Recruitment direct but also via agencies. Speculative applications may be successful if you contact the right person at the right time
Applications assessed after advertised closing dates and subject to strict internal processes.	Need to be much more proactive in seeking vacancies, not sending an application and waiting for an answer. Don't be afraid to circumvent the process.
Strict enforcement of equal opportunities policies with application processes designed to be fair to all applicants.	Application of policies at the discretion of the hiring manager. There can be opportuniuties to bypass the process through networking.
Applications usually submitted via a standard application form (SAF).	Application by CV and cover letter.
Formal assessment as to whether you meet the job specification.	Your ability to 'fit in', enthusiasm for the role and personal connections may override whether you have the proper qualifications for the job.
Salary will be pegged to national pay scales commensurate with your job title and responsibility, with little opportunity to negotiate.	Salary will be based on how much the company has budgeted for a position. If it is a senior role, total package may be entirely negotiable.
Continual monitoring of websites and public sector recruitment newspapers/ journals is the best way to find opportunities.	Networking and job sites are a more effective way to find opportunities.

Table 10.1

will be seeking people who are customer-focused: employees who can take on new expectations and responsibilities, work with partners and to very tight budgets. You'll need good IT, numeracy, written and communication skills. In leaner times, showing that you constantly seek service improvements and efficiencies will stand you in good stead. For more information, read Ben Makins' story on p.215.

PART 2: THE CV

We've been told that many recruiters spend no more than 30 seconds looking at a CV before coming to a decision. And most will only read the top third of your CV on a computer screen – that's all the opportunity you have to deliver a compelling message. This makes it even more of a challenge for the older jobseeker – how to impress in a short space and time when you have a long and impressive story to tell. There are countless specialist books that provide basic guidance on creating a CV. Our aim is to address the particular challenges faced by the mature jobseeker.

Your CV is your primary sales tool. It should present accurately and comprehensively what skills and capabilities you possess that make you the ideal candidate. It is not a life history or a career story. It has one purpose only – to make the reader want to meet you.

There are many different types of CV. If you're looking for employment you might use a 'functional', 'chronological' or 'hybrid' CV. Each has its own purpose. You might also need a 'summary' CV, as well as a full-length version. If you are applying for contract, consultancy or interim roles, you're likely to need a detailed CV that specifically describes the projects or assignments you have worked on. If you want to be self-employed you might need a 'bio' or 'profile' to send out when asked. All have a common purpose but are targeted at different audiences.

Whatever the format, your CV must be honest. Your skills and experience can be presented in the best possible light, but all the facts

– dates, responsibilities, job titles, company names – must be accurate. There are two reasons for this. The main one, of course, is that falsifying information on a CV is grounds for dismissal. In addition, you don't know where electronic copies of your CV might end up – it could be read by recruitment agencies, company HR departments, job boards and even your contacts. Nothing is guaranteed to lower your credibility more than someone coming across two CVs that make different claims for who you are and what you have done. Bear this in mind as you tailor your CV. Make sure the basic facts are accurate and honest.

CHECKLIST OF CV ESSENTIALS

If it's been some time since you wrote a CV, here's a reminder of the essential points to get right.

- Choose a 10pt to 12pt standard font that ensures your CV is readable on the majority of computers.
- Black text on a white background is still seen as the optimum combination for readability but also for printing and copying.
- Have each copy of your CV proofread by a partner, friend or coach. Check for spelling, grammar and punctuation.
- Where opinions differ on correct formatting, for example whether to capitalise the first letter in a bulleted list or not, decide what format you will follow and be consistent throughout.
- Write in the third person, not the first. Do not use 'I' in your CV.
- Your name and contact details should be on every page, in case the pages become separated after submission.
- Make sure your essential skills and experience are clearly visible to the reader, recognising that he or she may only spend seconds scanning your CV. The top third may be all that they read.
- Restrict yourself to two pages, or one if it is a summary or bio CV. Anything longer is highly unlikely to be read.

- Unless asked to do otherwise, save and submit your CV as a pdf file, thereby preventing accidental editing, or formatting shifts. If you know that a recruiter will edit your CV, ask to see a copy of what has been submitted on your behalf.

THE RIGHT CV FOR YOU

The person reading a CV is trying to decide whether you are worth interviewing. With this in mind, the presentational challenge for the older worker is twofold:

1. A career spanning decades is simply too much to describe in two pages.
2. There may be periods which are best 'glossed over': gaps that include a period of unemployment, or work in an industry that is not relevant to the position. Simply put, anything that encourages the perception that you are right candidate for the job should be included. Anything that detracts from that perception should be excluded.

A 'functional' CV places your skills and competencies on the first page, with employers and dates relegated to the second page if mentioned at all. This type of CV focuses on your skills and is most useful when these are more appropriate than a list of the jobs you have held. For example, if you are making a career change to a new industry, a functional CV will highlight the transferable skills you can offer, and it will give concrete examples.

A 'chronological' CV is the traditional format. All your previous jobs are listed in date order, starting with the most recent. This type of CV is most appropriate for someone seeking the next logical step on a career ladder. For example, a project manager who is looking to step up to a programme director position, or a sales director wanting a move to a board level position.

A mix of these two types is called a 'hybrid' CV. Your profile, skills and achievements are highlighted at the top of the CV, and then a chronological list of employers and jobs is provided further down. This is the best way to highlight your relevant skills, while not detracting from the fact that those skills are backed up by a considerable amount of experience with different companies. Of the three main CV types, the hybrid version is the most useful type for the mature jobseeker in our opinion and the one we recommend most often.

The sections of a typical hybrid CV are:

Page 1
  Profile
  Skills summary
  Employment history (summary)
Page 2
  Detailed employment history
  Education, professional development and memberships

A sample layout of a hybrid CV is shown at the end of this chapter. There will be occasions when a chronological or functional CV is required. Many recruiters still prefer chronological CVs so that they can see your career progression and compare your CV with others. You'll also find sample layouts of functional and chronological CVs at the end of the chapter.

You'll need as many CVs as jobs you are applying for. Every job application you make should be accompanied by a CV that is specifically tailored for that role. Given the ease of document editing, there is no reason to submit a 'stock' CV for an advertised position where you know what the recruiter wants.

CREATING THE CONTENTS OF YOUR HYBRID CV

Refer to your self-assessment for a comprehensive review of your skills, competencies, experiences and achievements. You will use this to create all of the parts of your CV.

Profile

This is a short summary that describes you, what you offer and what you are looking for. For example:

A sales director with a track record of 17 years of successful sales and business development activities in the IT outsourcing sector in the Middle East. Now seeking a board level position in the UK with a growing IT outsourcing consultancy.

Your profile should be as attention-grabbing as possible but also clearly justified by the content in subsequent sections. It may take days or weeks to get right, but it's worth the effort because often it is the only part of your CV that the recruiter reads. The profile should be tailored to the job.

Skills summary

This section should provide a concise overview of your skills, competencies and achievements. It allows you to highlight those that are relevant to the role, regardless of when you acquired them. From your self-assessment in Chapter 4, combine your skills and experience into factual statements such as:

Planning and Organising: A PRINCE2 Practitioner with 15 years of programme management experience in the financial services arena with [bank 1, bank 2]. Managed programmes up to £100m in annual value.

In this section you should also identify relevant vocational and technical qualifications (e.g. MCSP, CCIE, Lean Six Sigma Green Belt) that might be essential attributes for the role. If the recruiter is seeking someone with qualification XYZ and you have that, then include it in this section and not at the bottom of page two.

The skills section is where you put any keywords that employers or recruiters will be looking for, such as *leadership, staff, SAP, PRINCE 2, IBM, director, planning, implementation, board-level, entrepreneur, business development, sales.* It's important because CVs can now be scanned electronically for keywords.

Employment history

The person reading your CV will expect to see a chronological list of the jobs you have done, with the most recent appearing first. List the job title, the employer's name and from/to dates. In a hybrid CV we recommend doing this in two parts:

- on the first page, include a summary list of employers, showing just the company name, job title and dates of employment;
- on page two, include a more detailed listing showing the responsibilities you held and any achievements. This will probably fill most of the second page.

When describing each role, ask yourself: 'What is specifically relevant to the job I am applying for now?' Concentrate on describing only the pertinent aspects. Be as factual as possible. In general, the more recent the job, the greater the detail should be. When describing the role, focus on what you did, using action words rather than describing the role itself. For example, *Responsible for improving product quality by 25 per cent over a two-year period by leading a comprehensive company-wide overhaul of the quality assurance process* is much more impressive than stating: *Senior member of quality control function, was responsible for defining processes and procedures as well as implementation thereof.*

In most cases, detailed descriptions of positions you held more than 10 years ago are unlikely to be relevant. Some jobseekers will summarise these experiences under a separate heading, 'Earlier career', and simply list the employers. This illustrates the breadth of career experience you bring while acknowledging that a junior sales role in retail 15 years ago is not hugely relevant to your employment today.

Education, professional development and memberships

Relevance is doubly important here. Typically you would include details of university degrees but not O and A level results. Include any technical training you undertook that led to a vocational qualification (Cisco CCIE) but not all the management training courses (presentation skills, time management, etc.). List membership of professional institutions (accountancy, law, engineering, IOD) but not your membership of a model railway club (unless you know the recruiter is also a member).

Other information

You may include other information that is important for the recruiter to know. This may include: technical and/or business publications; papers or books; professional or personal interests that are relevant, e.g. president of the local chamber of commerce or rugby club; a language ability or sporting achievement, e.g. Olympic gold-medal winner, or national representative.

Don't be overly forthcoming with your interests outside work, unless they illustrate a relevant skill. For example, if you are applying for a management role in a leisure centre, the fact you are chairman of the local rugby club in your spare time is relevant: it demonstrates your community spirit and skills in sports management. But if you are applying for an IT consultant role that requires lots of international travel, it is not.

What NOT to include in a CV?

Remove all details that reveal your age – there is no need for this information. This doesn't just refer to your date of birth. Don't put dates against your qualifications. Likewise there is no need to reveal any details about your ethnic origin, religion, sexuality, political affiliation or marital status.

FREQUENTLY ASKED CV QUESTIONS

Our experience at the Job Club is that older workers are faced with certain challenges that require a more specific approach.

How do I deal with career gaps?

Don't hide them – be honest about why they occurred, but don't draw attention to them. By a career gap we mean a period on your CV when you were not in employment. A typical example might be a person who, after redundancy, made childcare or parental duties his or her prime focus for a period of time. On balance it's best to state this honestly but also to highlight any voluntary or part-time responsibilities you took on at this time, if it's relevant to the work you are applying for. Recognise also that, whatever the reason for your career gap, an employer who is looking for a specialist in a certain field, when faced with two candidates – one who has worked full-time in their chosen field for the last ten years and the other who has considerable experience but has been a stay-a-home parent for the last four years – will most likely choose the former as their skills will be more up to date. This is not discrimination but just common sense. However, there will be employers who recognise the advantages of taking on employees who have been through the parenting or childcare career gap and will see that as a positive.

How do I convince an employer I can make a career change?

The mature jobseeker may have a number of career changes on his or her CV or be hoping to make one. There are two challenges to consider – how to present past changes in a coherent way on your CV and, if you're planning a change, how to justify why you should be considered for a role in your new career field. In both cases, career specialists point to the concept of transferable skills. What skills did you use across different careers that are an indication of your strengths and capabilities in any role? What skills did you use in past roles that will be an asset in a new career? When creating your CV, highlight those skills in the top third of the first page. The functional CV wins out over the chronological and hybrid CVs in this case as it allows the career-changer to point clearly to transferable skills. Once the reader understands you have the skills to do the job, then you can go on to describe your employment history and achievements.

How do I list qualifications: academic, vocational, etc?

It's important to recognise that all qualifications have a limited time of relevance. Clearly they have a longer shelf life if they directly relate to the job offered. A long list of management or technical training courses attended more than ten years ago is best left off your CV. At this stage in your career, your recent training or a skills upgrade is more relevant. Be ruthless when pruning old qualifications from your CV.

How far back in time do I go with my employment history?

A good compromise is to include fewer details the further you go back chronologically on your CV. For jobs held over ten years ago, simply state the role title and employer. For jobs more than 15 years old, add the title 'Early Career' and list the industry or the employer if it's a household name.

How long should I make my CV?

Accepted wisdom is that two pages is the maximum length. A one-pager is sometimes useful when sending a speculative application. In some sectors and situations it might be appropriate to use a longer format. For example, a consultant or an IT contractor might list all the assignments they have had, and a research scientist might include a list of scientific papers they have authored. However, for most management and professional positions, recruiters and employers would see an overly long CV as evidence of poor writing skills and an inability to present information concisely. You can always include extra information as an appendix. Examples of your work, case studies of situations you have managed, lists of published papers, an account of project success could all be included as appendices. Ask whether the recipient is interested in seeing them before sending.

SUMMARY

The outcome of a successful application is not a job – it's an interview. If your application has been successful you will have left your potential employer with the impression that you may be the perfect candidate. They have a document that describes what you can do and how you meet the requirements of the role. They are excited that their problem (the vacancy) is about to be solved. In the next chapter we tell you how to continue to build this impression through the interview.

PAGE ONE

Name
Occupation or Profession

Address
Telephone
E-mail

Profile

Summary profile statement that describes you, your key achievements, what you bring to the workplace, how you work and mentions your career objective.

Skills summary

List the skills that you bring in relation to the role you are applying for, mentioning under each skill specific achievements or notable occasions when you used those skills.

Summary employment history (in reverse chronological order)

<from>	<to>	<employer>	<job title>
<from>	<to>	<employer>	<job title>
<from>	<to>	<employer>	<job title>
<from>	<to>	<employer>	<job title>
<from>	<to>	<employer>	<job title>

PAGE TWO

Detailed employment history (in reverse chronological order)

<from>   **<to>**   **<employer>**   **<job title>**

Short description of each employer's business.

List your responsibilities and achievements at each employer.

<from>	**<to>**	**<employer>**	**<job title>**
<from>	**<to>**	**<employer>**	**<job title>**
<from>	**<to>**	**<employer>**	**<job title>**
<from>	**<to>**	**<employer>**	**<job title>**

Earlier career

For employment more than 10–15 years ago, summarise positions and employers.

Education, qualifications and memberships

<qualification>	<institution or college>
<qualification>	<institution or college>

Name   Telephone   E-mail

Table 10.2   Hybrid CV Format

PAGE ONE

Name
Occupation or Profession

Address
Telephone
E-mail

Profile

Summary profile statement that describes you, your key achievements, what you bring to the workplace, how you work and mentions your career objective.

Skills summary

Describe the transferable skills that you bring in relation to the role you are applying for, mentioning under each skill specific achievements or notable occasions when you used this skill.

Skill 1

Skill 2

Skill 3

Skill 4

PAGE TWO

Detailed employment history (in reverse chronological order)

\<from\>   \<to\>   \<employer\>   \<job title\>

Short description of each employer's business.

List your responsibilities and achievements at each employer.

\<from\>	**\<to\>**	**\<employer\>**	**\<job title\>**
\<from\>	**\<to\>**	**\<employer\>**	**\<job title\>**
\<from\>	**\<to\>**	**\<employer\>**	**\<job title\>**
\<from\>	**\<to\>**	**\<employer\>**	**\<job title\>**

Earlier career

For employment more than 10–15 years ago, summarise positions and employers

Education, qualifications and memberships

\<qualification\>   \<institution or college\>
\<qualification\>   \<institution or college\>

Name   Telephone   E-mail

Table 10.3 Functional CV Format

PAGE ONE

Name   Address
                                                Telephone
Occupation or Profession   E-mail

Profile

Summary profile statement that describes you, your key achievements, what you bring to the workplace, how you work and mentions your career objective.

Employment history (in reverse chronological order)

\<from\>   \<to\>   \<employer\>   \<job title\>

Short description of employer's business.

List your responsibilities and achievements at this employer.

\<from\>   \<to\>   \<employer\>   \<job title\>

Short description of employer's business.
List your responsibilities and achievements at this employer.

PAGE TWO

Employment history (cont'd)

\<from\>   \<to\>   \<employer\>   \<job title\>

Short description of employer's business.

List your responsibilities and achievements at this employer.

\<from\>   \<to\>   \<employer\>   \<job title\>

Continue to cover at least 10 years of employment.

\<from\>	**\<to\>**	**\<employer\>**	**\<job title\>**
\<from\>	**\<to\>**	**\<employer\>**	**\<job title\>**
\<from\>	**\<to\>**	**\<employer\>**	**\<job title\>**

Earlier career

For employment more than 10–15 years ago, summarise positions and employers.

Education, qualifications and memberships

\<qualification\>   \<institution or college\>
\<qualification\>   \<institution or college\>

Name   Telephone   E-mail

Table 10.4 Chronological CV Format

THE INTERVIEW

There is no such thing as a bad interview, only a badly-prepared candidate. An interview is a key milestone in the job-search process. It's an opportunity for the employer and prospective employee to evaluate each other. The employer wants to determine if the candidate will be able to perform the role and fit into the existing office culture. The candidate wants to know if the workplace is congenial and if the job will provide satisfaction. So an interview can only have a positive outcome in that both parties have the chance to gather more information before coming to a more informed decision. If an employer decides not to proceed, it does not mean the candidate has failed, only that the employer has decided that person is not right for the role. The candidate may also decide, after the interview, that this is not the job for him or her.

The employer's decision is based on the impression the candidate makes at the interview, which should complement what is written on the CV. The strength of this impression will depend on how well-prepared the candidate is and how well they perform on the day. In some ways the interview is an act: the candidate turns up to put on a 'show' for his prospective employer. Any actor will tell you that a good performance is dependent on thorough preparation, and it's the same for an interview. Of course, the employer also has to prepare to run the interview, although sometimes there is little evidence of this. In this chapter we discuss preparation and execution from the candidate's perspective.

You may not have had a proper interview in years. It's quite possible to move from job to job via internal interviews and finding work through network contacts. Suddenly having to re-enter the job market via a formal interview process can come as a shock, so we will try to cover all the bases.

By 'interview' we mean the *entire* employer-to-candidate assessment-related process that takes place after the application. It follows the decision to meet the candidate, and precedes the moment when an offer is received. The interview process is not a one-off meeting. It happens over a period of time, during which one of more of the following will occur: telephone interviews and conversations; online assessment; a case study; selection panels; informal chats or meetings; first or 'screening' interview; follow-up interviews; and the final interview. Some of these may not take place directly with the employer but with a third party, a recruiter or consultant operating on the employer's behalf. With the company, an interview may be conducted by HR, by the hiring manager, a colleague or a senior executive.

If you are in the interview process this means the employer likes something about you, thinks you are a potential fit and would be happy if you turned out to be the ideal candidate. Remember, the whole selection process starts with a business problem: a vacancy that needs filling. The employer has shortlisted you because they consider it a possibility that you are the solution to the problem. You begin from a position of strength.

A well-run selection process is designed to find the best candidate, but even the best process is sometimes run by non-expert interviewers and recruiters. As a candidate, you will have to manage your way around poorly-asked questions, disorganised company departments, reluctant recruiters and uninspired executives. Remember that you are not there to judge the interview process; you are there to impress.

Take one step at a time. The objective of a CV is to get an interview, and the objective of each interview stage is simply to move to the next step. If it's a screening interview, you must concentrate your efforts and perform well enough to get on to the final shortlist. If you are asked to meet a potential colleague for an 'informal chat', treat it as just one more step and prepare accordingly. Do your research and know what type of candidate they want. Never assume that it's in the bag until you have a job offer in your hands, and always concentrate your efforts on getting past the next hurdle.

TYPES OF INTERVIEW

There is more than one kind because over time, employers have refined, and continue to refine, the interviewing process to make it more effective. The number of stages in the process will depend on the size of organisation and the seniority of the role being filled. When interviewing for a senior role in an SME, the interview process will likely consist of a series of meetings with functional directors and perhaps a final chat with the MD, after which a collective decision is made whether or not to make an offer. The interview process for a middle-management role in a large corporate may follow a rigid, well-defined series of steps: 1. Initial interview 2. Personality profile and numerical reasoning tests 3. Competency interview 4. Senior manager interview. After each step you are informed if you have passed.

The initial screening interview

The purpose of this is to meet you and determine whether it is worth investing any more time in you. The desired outcome is that you move forward to the next stage of the process. The interviewer is checking that the view they formed of you from your CV is correct, as well as other aspects that don't come through on the CV: your ability to speak clearly and articulate a point of discussion, the impression you give, and your level of confidence in your abilities. The goal in this interview is to deliver on the promise of your CV. By this time you'll have a clear idea how well your skills match the brief. Don't introduce complications like salary or place of work into the discussion. Do rehearse the stories of your achievements so that you speak credibly and confidently, demonstrating your capabilities and ensuring that these are related to, and confirm, what is on your CV.

Competency interview

This method of interviewing is based on the principle that the best predictor of how a person will apply their skills in future work situations is their behaviour in similar situations in the past. Rather than ask about your experiences and achievements, the competency interview focuses on situations you were placed in and how you used your skills to make progress. The situations don't have to be related to the greatest achievements in your career – often the best examples of how effectively you used your skills come from times of adversity rather than triumph. So interviewers will ask questions like:

> *'Can you tell me about a time when you felt you were the only one in your department or management team who had the "right" answer to a problem. How did you go about enrolling others in your approach?'*

> *'Can you give me an example of a time when you had to make a very unpopular decision? How did you arrive at the decision? How did you communicate it?'*

You could be asked some very challenging questions. The interviewer is trying to determine how you apply your skills in the situation and is not particularly interested in the business outcome. When answering, focus on your own skills and actions rather than the company or team. The interviewer is interested in your competencies, not the team's achievement or the company's progression. Think in terms of *I did...I decided...I thought...I told...I argued that...I persuaded... I presented...I asked...I bought...I sold...*

The best way to prepare for competency-based interviews is to make sure you understand the key skills required and then practise answering questions around those skills. Note that a competency-based interview may be a specific part of the interview process, or the interviewer might use some competency-based questions in a more general interview. The technique is now widely used, and it's best to always prepare for competency-based questions.

Functional interview

The purpose is very simple: Can you do the job? The employer seeks to understand whether you have the technical and/or management skills to do what is required in the role. They are checking you have done what it says on your CV.

It's important to be clear about what you did and how you did it, to show how you applied your skills and to demonstrate a thorough knowledge of those areas in which you claim to be an expert. Prepare by studying your subject matter. Practise by speaking to other experts on the topic and update yourself on the latest technical trends. You should be able to speak confidently about any technical subject areas on your CV.

Panel interview

Here you are interviewed by more than one person simultaneously. There are several reasons for this: it may be company policy, or a number of departments may have to reach a collective decision on a candidate. Your challenge is to prepare to meet more than one person and build rapport with the group. If a panel interview is run well there should only be one person asking questions at any one time. You need to concentrate your efforts on answering that question. If two or more people ask questions at once, it's perfectly acceptable to ask which one you should answer first, or state that you will answer first one then the other. It may be that the company wants to find out how you cope with being the centre of attention in a board meeting, and they are testing your ability to manage communication with a challenging group. If you are invited to a panel interview, ask what the nature of the interview will be (e.g. questions from separate people with different functional expertise, or a challenging board style interview as described above) and request the names of the individuals who will be on the panel and their job titles. Be prepared to be exhaustively examined on all aspects of your CV, as one questioner will pick up from another.

The telephone interview

This is a great way for a recruiter or employer to save travel time for all concerned. In some cases, if the interviewee and interviewer are in different countries it may be the only possible way to conduct an interview in a reasonable time frame or at reasonable cost. There are a number of simple principles to bear in mind for telephone interviews because all the non-verbal communication that normally takes places in a conversation cannot happen. The interviewer will form an impression about you through your tone of voice, clarity of enunciation, your accent, and how you order and structure your answers. It's important to speak slowly and coherently and make an effort to match the pace of the interviewer. Keep your responses short where possible and always check for understanding. In a face-to-face interview you receive messages from body language and facial expressions as to whether your answers are hitting the right buttons; in a telephone interview you must be alert for changes in tone and pace that indicate whether or not you have answered a question correctly.

Treat it like a business meeting. Make sure you are alone in a setting or location where you can concentrate on the interview and where you won't be disturbed. A telephone interview requires a high level of concentration. You will need to have the same documents to hand that the interviewer does, including CV, job specification and any other information about the role. This will minimise any misunderstandings about you and the role being discussed. These could be easily cleared up when meeting face-to-face but could get quite complicated on the phone.

At the end of the call, it's worth being explicit regarding subsequent steps. Ask what will happen next, and by when. You might probe the interviewer for a brief summation of their conclusions. It's acceptable to ask: 'How do you think that went? Will you want to see me or speak to me again?'

Final interview

This is the last hurdle before that elusive job offer. Sometimes you will have a clear set of instructions to follow. You might be asked to present your case to the board or a senior manager. It's usually established that a decision will be made immediately after the meeting.

At other times the final interview is called something else. For example, you might be told: 'We just want you to have a chat with the managing director before we make you an offer.' Beware – this is not 'just a chat', it's a final check as to whether or not they think you will fit in.

By the time you get to a final interview you will have researched the company and the role and you will know why they think you're a suitable candidate. In a final interview, reiterate your strengths and demonstrate again how you will bring value to the role, building on what you have already said at previous interviews. At this stage it's yours to lose. Bear in mind this is also your last opportunity to interview them. Do you have all the information you need to make a decision? If not, now is the time to ask.

OTHER ELEMENTS OF THE INTERVIEW PROCESS

Personality and aptitude tests

These are designed to create a profile of how you operate in life and work, so you can be compared to the profiles of other people applying for the role. There are no right or wrong answers, and it is very difficult, even if you suspect you know what sort of personality traits the role requires, to fool the tests. They come from reputable suppliers. Tests include embedded questions to check for honesty and integrity in the responses. You'll jeopardise your chances by attempts to second-guess your responses.

If you have not done these tests before or for some time, it is a good idea to do a few test papers (available on line from SHL: **www.shl. com**) to get into the right mindset. The tests may be administered in person by an interviewer, in your own office or online. For online tests you will be sent a logon to the test provider's site by the company. When it is time to take the actual test you need to be in a work frame of mind. Be calm and focused so the results are a picture of you at your best. Results may be e-mailed to you but it's more likely that the company will receive a copy and discuss them with you at an interview.

Verbal and numerical reasoning tests

These examine your problem-solving and decision-making capabilities. Based on statistical data, optimum results for specific roles are compiled and your scores will be compared to them. This helps the employer to judge how well you are likely to perform in the role. In contrast to personality tests, there are definitely right and wrong answers, and we recommend you do some trial tests in advance. Your recruiter may be able to supply sample tests or you can find some online. Doing cryptic crosswords, sudoku and mental arithmetic are other ways to prepare for these tests.

Case studies

A case study is a common way for employers to test the clarity of your thinking, your analytical skills, and your ability to present a case for action. Typically you will be given a scenario to evaluate. It could be presented on a written document, a DVD or a website, and you might receive a verbal briefing. You will be given a fixed time to analyse the situation and present your findings and recommendations to the interviewer. It may require a short presentation or involve cooperating with other interviewees. There is no specific online resource for practising for case studies. A well-established company may have an archive of case studies that you can research, but otherwise, be yourself and respond as you would if you were in the job.

PREPARATION FOR INTERVIEWS

As a mature worker, you have the advantage of being well-versed in the rules of business and the importance of preparation for any meeting. Companies and interviewers often report how surprised they are at the lack of preparation by interviewees. So learn as much as you can about the company, their services and reputation, why they're adding staff, and what challenges they face. If this information is not available online, use your network to contact people who know about the company. At the interview you want to be to able to speak coherently about what the company does. Use social and business networking sites to research the people you will meet. What are their interests and backgrounds? Where did they last work? How long have they been with the company? This could be valuable information when you make small talk initially, and it may offer clues about the employer's ideal candidate.

You cannot afford for your early interviews to be practice sessions, because you might miss a great opportunity, so make sure you practise well beforehand. Either find a willing partner or colleague, or seek professional help – many career guidance and career coaching companies will offer a test interview service, where you attend a mock interview based on the real job description and give the interviewer a copy of your application. Top services will provide you with a video recording of the interview and a summary with feedback on how you came across, identify your strengths and your weaknesses, and how well you match the impression given by your CV.

In the book *What Color Is Your Parachute?*[1], Richard N. Bolles notes that all the interview questions in the world can be summarised in just five questions you have to be able to answer when going to any interview. As two of them are similar we have listed just four 'big questions' below. All the other questions you will be asked will relate in some way to these four: 1. Why do you want this job? 2. Can you do the job? 3. Why are you the best candidate? 4. Will you fit in here? Be prepared to answer them at any stage in the interview process – some might come up at an initial interview and then be repeated in more depth as you go through the process. You need to have a 30-second 'elevator pitch' response to these questions, with a more detailed answer prepared as well, one that includes evidence and will back up your brief answer. In other words, the elevator pitch functions as a kind of executive summary for a much longer answer.

1. Why do you want this job?

No company wants to employ someone who is only doing the job because there was nothing else on offer or because the package sounded good. This is a recipe for disaster. Once the novelty of being employed in the new role or having a higher income has worn off, what will keep the employee motivated and engaged? Extensive research points to job satisfaction, opportunities for development and good management as the top reasons why people remain in a role. Salary and benefits are always way down the list. At the interview, the company is looking for evidence that you have good reasons for wanting this job and that these will match what they can offer you in the medium to long term. Think through what it is about the role and the company that means this would be a good move for you. You want to be able to express this as a win-win, not just in terms of what you can get out of it. Here's an example of a short, elevator-pitch answer:

'I want this job because my experience in this sector means I can focus my efforts from day one on developing new revenue streams for this business unit. I'm also excited that senior roles might exist in future, because the company is growing fast and has a good reputation as a place to work.'

2. Can you do the job?

If you convince the employer that you want the job, the next consideration is whether you can do it. To find the answer to this question, the interviewer will focus on exploring the relevant experience from your CV and also the 'soft' skills that may not be apparent from the CV but are just as important. Technical skills can be judged by tests (e.g. verbal and numerical reasoning tests) or case studies. Soft skills are explored with competency questions as well as personality and aptitude tests.

The skills you need for the job are found in the job description. Prepare for this question by making a list of relevant experience and qualifications that demonstrate that you can perform above expectations. Where you have an obvious gap, acknowledge it and describe how you will address it.

This question is often the first one an interviewer will use to create a shortlist of candidates based on CV analysis. By the time you get to the interview, the recruiter already considers you can do the job. The interviewer is now looking for further evidence to make a stronger case for you. Your answers to questions relating to this point should therefore back up what is already on your CV. Be well-rehearsed.

3. Why are you the best candidate?

Another way to phrase this is: *'You want the job and I see you can do it but so can 20 other people, so why should I choose you?'* This is difficult to answer, because you can't compare yourself to your competition. You can only make your strongest case based on what you know about the role and the company. This is where your maturity and experience as an older jobseeker come into play. If you can show that you are fully aware of what the job entails and you are able to demonstrate insights into the challenges you might face, you will stand out from the crowd. Describe similar roles you have done in the past and what the critical success factors were in the first hundred days of employment and also in the first year. Seek to demonstrate your value proposition. Ask intelligent questions that demonstrate your expertise.

If the interview is for a senior role, the interviewer has half an eye on where you might move within the organisation – for example, have you the potential to be the next CFO or COO? The more potential value you can offer, the more likely you are to stand out from others. On the other hand, you may be interviewed for a junior role – a step down from your previous status – so you'll need a convincing rationale. You'll have to explain why it makes career sense for you to take this role now. Valid reasons are: a move into a new industry, career change, a desire to improve your work/life balance, or a specific objective. See Michael's story (p.184) for an example of how this can be done.

You can prepare for the 'best candidate' question and the 'why do you want this job?' question simultaneously by listing 10 strengths you have that are relevant to the role. Decide which of these allow you to do the job well, and which offer future opportunities to the employer. Emphasise the latter at the interview.

4. Will you fit in here?

This is potentially the hardest question for the older worker. As we mentioned in the first chapter, if success in the job depends on fitting in with a young team, your chances are not very good. If this is a role where the need for your technical expertise outweighs any concerns the employer has about age, then you stand a chance. You cannot rely on government legislation to protect you from exclusion on the grounds that you do not fit in.

Don't bang your head against a brick wall. Find employers who value what you can bring to the organisation. When being interviewed, don't be afraid to ask the direct question: *'Do you think I will fit in here?'* Listen for the answers. You have a chance to sell yourself if you engage in a dialogue about the issue. There is no longer an 'elephant in the room' because the age issue is out in the open. There will be situations where age is genuinely not an issue. In this case you can only answer honestly to questions about your working style and how you like to be managed. The personality tests you have undertaken will have given the employer clues as to your fit with the role. How you perform at interview complements this view.

Be aware there are other ways to determine fit. Some employers will ask off-the-wall questions designed to see what sort of person you are outside of work: *'If money was no object, what car would you drive? If you had an extra day a week for the rest of your life what would you do with the time? Which three famous people, alive or dead, would you choose to join you for your fiftieth birthday party?'* These questions are designed to form a better picture of the person you really are and how that might affect your ability to work with other people in the team. For example, if you answered the car question with *'a Ford Focus Estate because it's practical for my current lifestyle',* and the rest of the management team pride themselves on their luxury four-wheel drives, then however well you could do the job, you just might not fit in!

The secondary element to the 'fit' question relates to salary. Your fit in terms of salary is just as important as your personality fit. *'Are you too expensive for us?'* is a real concern for a small company hiring someone with a corporate background. Be honest and up front about what your negotiating range is; it's best for both parties to find out early whether this is going to be a waste of time if the company is unable to match your salary expectations.

THE SEVEN KILLER QUESTIONS

In addition to the four big questions, there are seven killer questions that you must be ready for. We can't offer answers as they will be particular to your situation. Think through them and practise your responses.

1. Why have you been looking for work for so long?
2. Why were you made redundant?
3. How long will you want to work here?
4. What have you been doing while out of work?
5. What are your aspirations for the next five or ten years?
6. Why does your CV look like it does (one employer in 25 years or 20 employers in 25 years)?
7. What makes you think you can make the change from self-employment back into corporate employment again?

MANAGING THE INTERVIEW

It's worth reiterating some of the essential points that are easy to overlook if you have not been to an interview for some time.

Time

Allow plenty of time in order to arrive early at the interview. If you cannot attend or decide not to, in the interests of networking make your reasons clear and inform the company or the agent.

CV

The interviewer may not have seen your CV until you arrive. You might think your CV has been pored over and analysed in great detail, but it is quite possible for the interviewer to either be reading your CV while interviewing you, or never to have seen it at all. So always take two copies with you and be prepared to draw attention to the points relevant to your application.

Dress code

The rule here is simple – always dress to impress as if you were doing the job. If you are applying for a job in a company where casual clothing is the norm, then very smart casual or even a suit might be appropriate. If it's a company where suits are still the order of the day, then a new shirt and clean tie are definitely recommended. Always remember: if you were working at this place, what would you wear to impress? If it's not clear, than ask the recruitment agent or the employer directly.

Rapport

The initial part of the interview, like any meeting between strangers, is where rapport is established. Rapport means that you are connecting with the other person. It's important to remember when meeting a person for an interview that you are a guest in their world. You can build rapport by conforming easily to the rules they have set up for the interview: *You sit there and I sit here. I ask the questions initially and then you ask some later. I want to tell you about my company before you start talking. I want to hear you speak about your journey here while I get comfortable.* You can break rapport early on by deliberately flouting the rules the interviewer is trying to impose, or by seeking to take control of the conversation.

Other simple rules for establishing good rapport are to use the interviewer's language or jargon where possible, and to mirror their posture without being obvious. If they are sitting upright, forward and with both hands on the table, then you should too. If they start using technical terms to describe an aspect of the role, then include those terms in your answer. Reply to short succinct questions with a brief answer.

Speaking and listening

It's very easy to half-listen, especially when being interviewed for a job for which you are highly qualified. You might find yourself mentally preparing to answer the question you think should have been asked rather than the one you actually were asked. Listening carefully is doubly important if you think the interviewer knows less about the topic than you. Answer the question as asked, showing your experience where possible, and focusing on the thought that you are here to pass the interview and not to intimidate the interviewer.

When speaking, try to avoid giving a longer answer than the interviewer is expecting. Again, with your experience, it might be possible for you to give a competent 15-minute answer to an open question about how you would approach the role. However, unless asked to give a presentation, you should limit the length of your answers to what would be appropriate in a conversation.

Answering difficult or unexpected questions

Despite all your preparation, you will sometimes face an unexpected or difficult question. Some interviewers will deliberately plan these questions to see how you react, others will simply be obvious to the interviewer but ones you didn't expect. Either way, rather than stammer or rush in with an ill thought-out answer, the best approach is to:

Pause – don't feel you have to answer immediately; you might even say: 'I'll need a couple of seconds to think about that.'

Breathe – take a breath while you gather your thoughts.

Think – ask yourself what the interviewer is trying to achieve with this question. What examples or knowledge can you call on to find an answer that best fits with what they want to hear?

Speak – confidently and assertively, looking out for clues in the interviewer's body language as to whether or not you are on the right track.

Material to leave

It is sometimes appropriate to take examples of your previous work to the interview and to show or leave this as evidence of your capabilities. If so, make sure that you have checked with someone else first that the items are of good quality and convey the right impression. A market research report that you wrote might have been fit for purpose by the standards of the small family-run company you worked for, but could appear amateurish when judged by the standards of a multinational. The reverse could also be true – examples of your work with a large corporate could appear overly complex and theoretical if you are interviewing for a role with a three-person start-up company.

Asking questions

Any interview process should allow you the opportunity to ask questions. You are also conducting your own interview – *'Is this company one I want to work for? Will I fit in? Will I get the opportunities I want?'* It's best to prepare your questions in advance to ensure that all the points important to your decision will be covered.

HOW LONG SHOULD I WAIT FOR A RESPONSE AFTER AN INTERVIEW?

Ask this question *before* you leave the interview. A professional approach means establishing the next steps before you leave. Will they contact you? Directly or through an agent? By when?

It's good practice to send a thank-you e-mail after the interview and within 24 hours. You might follow up on any outstanding points and reiterate your interest in the role. If you haven't been told when you'll hear of the outcome, we recommend following up with the agent within a day, or directly with the employer within three days.

POST-INTERVIEW REVIEW

After every interview you attend, you should make notes about how you performed. Each interview is another opportunity to learn about how you come across when applying for work. A bad interview will teach you more about yourself than a good one. As soon as possible after the interview, note down answers to the following questions:

- How did I do?
- Which questions did I answer particularly well?

- Which questions did I answer particularly badly?
- What did I learn about how I present myself?
- What did I learn about the company?
- In summary, what did I learn about my interviewing skills that I can take forward to the next one?

If it's possible to get feedback from the company or the recruiter who put you forward, take the opportunity to do so. By analysing the feedback you receive, you will be better prepared for the next one. When reviewing feedback, remember that most people tend to be cautious about what feedback they offer, for fear of giving offence. So it's important to note the trends and unspoken messages in the feedback you're getting. For example, if all the responses are positive but most interviewers hint at your slightly 'direct' nature, then consider whether you are coming across as too aggressive in the interviews. Act on any consistent trends in the feedback you receive.

NEXT STEPS

After every interview there are three possible outcomes:

1. You've passed and you move on to next step in the interview process. Excellent! It's now time start your preparation for what is to come.
2. Rejection. It's always disappointing to be rejected. Treat every rejection as one more learning step in the process towards finding the ideal role.
3. You got a job offer. Great! Fantastic, well done!

Before you celebrate, wait to see the offer in writing. Now is the time to think about what you want from the role and whether there is scope for negotiation. The point at which you are made an offer is the point at which your negotiating power is highest. The company has decided that they want you. There is a more than reasonable chance that you are motivated to do well and will fit in. Now is the time for you to be clear about your salary, benefits, reporting lines, job title and so on.

A full review of all the aspects of negotiating your terms of employment is beyond the scope of this book. However, it's worth mentioning that you also have to gauge how open the company is to negotiation. What alternatives do they have if you are insisting on a higher salary or certain conditions? If you really are the only person that can do the role, then hold out for what you want. If other potential candidates are still available, be careful about how you position your requirements. Make clear that you are not threatening to withdraw; you only want to secure the right offer for the role.

SUMMARY

An interview can be daunting, especially if you have not been interviewed for some time. There are several steps in a process which you and the potential employer will go through to assess your suitability for the role. Through adequate preparation and practice you can give yourself the best possible chance of success. Aim to walk out of every interview having left the best possible impression. The final decision is always with the interviewer, but you'll want to be able to say: 'I did my best. Now it's up to them.'

SUCCESS STORY: MICHAEL

One of the hardest things to do is sell yourself *down*. Most employers won't hire an experienced person to do a job that has lower status and pay than in their previous role. The assumption is that someone who is overqualified will get bored and leave quickly; that their motive for seeking the position is simply to get working again in order to have an income while they look for a better job. And yet many older workers would be happy to step down a level and do a job they enjoy, working in congenial surroundings for a company they respect. Michael's story is an example of how it can be done. It's also a heart-rending tale of a man who overcame one of the worst results of unemployment:

clinical depression. He asked us to conceal his identity, and that of his employers.

With a blue-chip education starting at public school, followed by an Oxbridge degree and an MBA, Michael was set for a promising career in corporate finance. Following a stint with a private equity firm in the City, he was taken on as a financial analyst by an industrial conglomerate. He was spotted as a future finance director, but the 1991 recession meant that there was no opportunity for progression within the company. After answering an advert in the *Financial Times*, he was recruited by a major telecoms firm, where he spent a decade in their corporate finance operation. He faced his first redundancy in 2002 in the media/telecoms recession that followed the bursting of the dotcom bubble in 2001. Michael was out of work for a mere six weeks, and then another advert in the FT helped him secure a senior role in project finance for another conglomerate. It was essentially the same job that he'd done previously. The company was sold in 2008 and so, at age 49, Michael faced his second, life-changing redundancy.

There was conflict with his former employer over his redundancy package. Anxiety about his situation led to constant sleepless nights, loss of appetite and dark moods. After four months he went to his doctor. The diagnosis was depression. He was sent away with recommendations for herbal remedies, over-the-counter soporifics, and self-help books. His depression was so severe that none of the remedies, or the advice, was of any use. He says four things helped him through this difficult period:

- Having no serious financial worries. His partner has a good salary and he had money saved.
- Caring for his young son, who has special needs. This gave him a powerful reason to get out of bed and face the day.
- Proper medication in the form of sleeping pills and antidepressants (they were finally prescribed).

- Therapy provided by the NHS, available through a programme for the unemployed.

Michael was out of work for 18 months. During that time he was always looking for a job. There was no 'lightbulb' moment of inspiration; it was sheer perseverance that got him through. And each time he faced an interview or networking meeting he 'pretended confidence'. 'We all do that, don't we?' he says.

Michael's new job didn't come through an advert in FT; it came from networking. A former colleague told him about a job that was being offered by a big multinational that had been refused by the applicant, so he knew they were recruiting. Through his network he got the name of the department head, spoke to him directly, and then went in for an informal chat. This was for a junior position, one with a much lower salary than what Michael had been accustomed to. His challenge was not to convince his future employer of his talent, but of his sincerity. He did it by being honest about his rationale, so that his employer could understand why he would be willing to take a step down. He had two convincing reasons:

- His son needed special care during the working day, something he was unable to provide adequately by himself. This family situation was believable to his employer.
- He was impressed by the company and has always wanted to work for them.

The employer was sold on the benefits of having Michael on board and he got the job. He likes the people he works with; he's proud that he sold himself down – it is a real achievement. And he agrees with his partner who told him, 'This job just might suit you.' Over time, he might try for a higher position in the company but the role will have to be right for him, his family and his lifestyle.

Move Forward:
Self-Employment

INTERIM MANAGEMENT

THE WORK FUNNEL

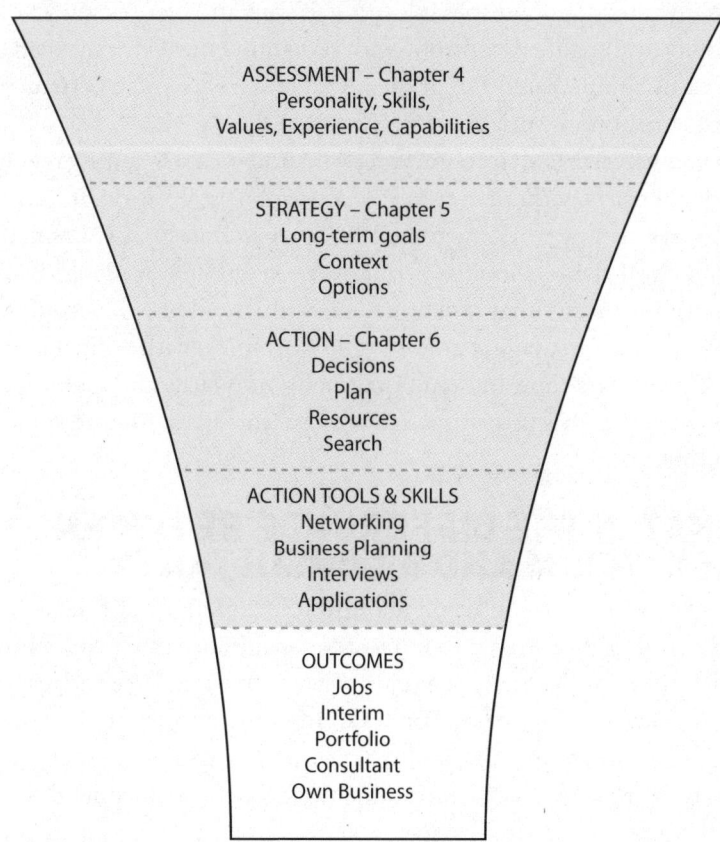

ASSESSMENT – Chapter 4
Personality, Skills,
Values, Experience, Capabilities

STRATEGY – Chapter 5
Long-term goals
Context
Options

ACTION – Chapter 6
Decisions
Plan
Resources
Search

ACTION TOOLS & SKILLS
Networking
Business Planning
Interviews
Applications

OUTCOMES
Jobs
Interim
Portfolio
Consultant
Own Business

WHAT IS AN INTERIM?

Interims are experienced senior managers and directors who are appointed temporarily, either in a functional role or to manage a short-term project. An interim will usually have board-level experience, be part of the management team and committed to its objectives, and then leave the company with an action plan in place, having completed a pre-agreed set of objectives.

This is one occupation where age is seen as an advantage. When an interim is required, most employers will seek an older person who is sensibly overqualified, someone with skills and knowledge that can be put to use immediately. All of the invisible age barriers to permanent employment now work in your favour.

If you succeed as an interim, you could find yourself getting regular work contracts without ever having a permanent position. It's also a good way to stay working at a senior level so that your CV remains current and viable, should a permanent role become available. Being an interim means that you're in line with trends in the economy. Employers are managing a more agile workforce, with an increasing number of part-time and temporary jobs. Similarly, at a senior level more work is being contracted out, so the need for interims is growing.

WHAT IS THE DIFFERENCE BETWEEN AN INTERIM AND A CONSULTANT?

There can be some confusion about the role of an interim manager and that of a consultant. To be clear: a consultant is someone who is hired (either individually or as part of a team) to diagnose and resolve a problem (which might, on examination, appear to be many problems), works to a timescale that could be expanded, resulting in a report that presents recommendations for someone else to implement. An interim is a doer, not an adviser, and an implementer, not a report writer. Interims will manage the solution to a problem or they will be the temporary replacement for a permanent manager. Interims work in the company office on a daily basis, whereas consultants are always external people. Consultants may be free to come and go, and to work from home – sometimes on several projects at once. Diagnostic skills are required in both roles, but the major difference is that interims are hands-on, whereas consultants typically examine and then offer advice, plans and proposals. Sometimes there are grey areas and overlap between the two roles.

WHY HIRE AN INTERIM?

Interims are employed for a variety of reasons: to implement the solution to an outstanding problem; manage a board-level project; or to fill a gap during recruitment. Crisis management is often a motive for hiring an interim: there may be a reorganisation or insolvency. An interim could also be used to assist with starting or closing a division, or to implement a new system. In essence, a company will hire an interim because they have a situation that requires immediate attention and they need a competent person who can step in and take charge. Interims will typically work from four to nine months; this may be full-time or three to four days per week. Longer assignments are possible. Some employers offer flexible contracts, such as 90 days in six months, which allow for periods of leave and the ebb and flow of workload in the role.

ARE YOU SUITED TO INTERIM MANAGEMENT?

Here's a short list of some characteristics that an interim should have:

- instant credibility;
- able to lead from the front;
- recent experience in the sector, typically at board or director level;
- up-to-date knowledge;
- experience with project management concepts – managing a set of activities that have a start and an end;
- impartiality;
- comes with no agenda (does not want a permanent job).

You must be a person who enjoys diversity and a challenge, someone who is able to get things going rapidly. And you must also be able to sell yourself in order to get contracts.

Interim management is not for everyone. If you value security and regularity more than the excitement of a new task, then it won't be suitable. Some other things to consider: starting out is not easy; gaps between jobs may be long (especially at the beginning); and you're responsible for your own continuing professional development. You'll be freelance, so you'll need to set up a personal services company that will carry an admin overhead. Pension and health insurance will be your responsibility.

Mike Taylor has worked as an interim and he has set up public sector interim divisions within two major agencies: Tribal and Boydens. Mike and his partners are currently running their own agency, Your Choice Interims. He offers excellent advice for anyone considering work as an interim, either in the public or the private sector. He says you should consider four questions:

1. Can you afford to be out of work for any period of time? Do you have a cushion? How long will it last?
2. Can you handle not living and working from home? Many assignments mean living in a hotel room for several months or travelling abroad, or there could be travel at the beginning and end of the working week so you can return home at weekends.
3. Can you think of yourself as a different entity and redefine yourself? Are you able to rewrite your CV to include transferable skills that work in your market?
4. Can you move flexibly into organisations? Are you outcome driven?

If you've answered yes to all these questions, we recommend that you discuss it with your family, or anyone who is reliant on you for income. Seek an objective perspective. Talk it over with a neutral third party, perhaps a career counsellor. Interim agencies such as Veredus run free seminars; you may want to take one to find out if this type of work will suit you. Mike recommends a one-day workshop offered by the IMA Institute. Details are found on their website: **www.ima-institute. com**.

HOW TO SET UP AS AN INTERIM

As with any new business, you'll need to define exactly what product or service you're selling. In this case, *you* are the product and your services are for sale. What is it that you do best? In which area of management have you been most successful? Write down your capabilities. Next, follow Mike Taylor's advice: 'Write your CV as if an ill-informed person were reading it. An interim CV is about abilities more than experience – concentrate on the outcomes of the roles you have completed.'

- **Express your core skills in plain language.**
- **Specify your skills and give evidence.**
- **Don't diminish the talents you take for granted.**
- **Don't assume that others will understand what your experience means.**

As an example of the final point above, all accountants have audit experience; therefore, all accountants assume that everyone knows that. But it may not be the case. HR can be uneven and your CV may be seen by a lower-level person. If that person doesn't know that all accountants have audit experience, they won't know that you possess an essential skill required for the role. If you haven't included it in your CV, you might be passed over in favour of someone who has.

When you've finished a draft CV, it's time to approach an agency. The interim sector is well established and there are many good ones. Once you've expressed your interest, there will be a follow-up phone call or a meeting, giving you a chance to establish a relationship and find out what openings there might be for you in the market. This will also provide you with an opportunity to get feedback on your CV, so that it can be revised as necessary. Mike suggests that you don't register with too many agencies; five or six will do for a start. We've listed some in the Resources section at the back of the book.

Next ask yourself: 'Where would my boss go if he was looking for me?' If it's an agency, then contact that agency. When companies want someone they frequently ask this question internally: 'Does anyone know someone?' That's why it's important to use your network and inform everyone that you're available. If you know an interim, or if you have a friend who can connect you with one, by all means have a meeting. First-hand knowledge is of great value when you're starting a new venture.

For most people, landing the first interim assignment is the biggest hurdle. Some agencies will only take people who have experience as an interim. Be tenacious and keep networking. If you've developed your list of contacts by working through the networking chapter, you may find someone who can help you with your first assignment; they can either hire you or recommend you (three or four enthusiastic referees are a must). Once you've done your first assignment you'll have an interim reference and then the agencies will take you seriously. In other words, your network could land you your first contract, which gets you the necessary interim experience so that an agency will take you on; after working on some agency assignments you may no longer need an agency because you are likely to get your contracts through your own network. Or you may find that you never use an agent (see Graham Stephens' story on p.197). In any case, you will trade on your reputation: every job builds your credibility for the next interim role.

If you haven't yet been made redundant, consider approaching your boss and offering to complete an outstanding project on a freelance basis; convert yourself into a private contractor before you leave. You could ask for it as part of your outsourcing package. If you succeed, it would be your first statement of independent activity.

WHAT DO YOU CHARGE?

Interim fees are determined by the market and most people charge themselves out on a day rate, and invoice monthly. There is a considerable variance of rates, depending on your functional area and the geographic region where you work. There are no hard and fast rules; the only guideline is to be good value for the money. To get your first assignment, you might undercut the competition on price, and attach a performance-related bonus to the contract.

IS A CONTRACT NECESSARY?

It's important to get a formal agreement, either a contract or a simple letter of agreement. Mike says that you must define ten key objectives when arriving as an interim. Get them in writing or have your agent include them in a contract before you start. That way you'll avoid any misunderstandings that could arise with regard to what's expected of you in the assignment. Mike describes this as the 'millstone in the middle of the table' syndrome: you're having meetings where some unresolved issue just lies there and it's not your responsibility, although other people may think it is. An agreement sorts that out beforehand.

MORE EXPERT ADVICE

Mike suggests that before you complete an assignment, ask for a testimonial and send it with your updated CV to all your agencies and contacts. Every contract adds 'interim value' and enhances your presentation of skills and abilities. Your next assignment could come a lot faster as a result.

Finally, never break a contract by leaving early. You will damage your reputation.

THE PAPERWORK

Paperwork is something to be reckoned with, but rest assured you're in good company; every self-employed, freelance person has to deal with admin. These are the essentials:

- set up as a limited company;
- opt out of Employment Agency Act (EAA) regulations;
- get professional indemnity insurance (as required);
- hire an accountant with IR35 one-man-company experience;
- register for VAT if necessary.

Companies only hire other companies for contract work. If an individual's tax status is challenged, the company is liable for any tax and National Insurance contributions (NICs) that are due. That's the first reason you need to set up as a limited company; the second is that interim managers are classified as temporary workers under employment regulations introduced in 2004, called the Employment Agency Act (EAA). The act was set up to protect temporary workers and give them some of the rights of permanent employees. With your company acting as contractor, you do not require those rights and so you will need to sign a letter or form whereby you opt out of EAA. Agents should provide the form for this as part of the contract material for an assignment. If not, ask for it. Opting out has the additional benefit of reinforcing your protection against IR35, another piece of legislation that impacts on the activities of free-lancers. IR35 was introduced in 2000 as an attempt by Inland Revenue to tax what is deemed to be 'disguised employment' at a rate similar to employment. There's no need to be frightened of these regulations; interims operate in a completely legal way. Interim managers are contractors, not employees. What you are doing is protecting yourself from legislation that was not designed for the interim and freelance sector as it effectively operates. At the time of writing, the government was reconsidering legislation affecting freelancers (including IR35), presumably with the intent to simplify matters. If you have questions, discuss them with an agent or seek advice from your accountant.

Professional indemnity insurance protects you against any suit that could be brought against you because of the actions you have taken as an interim. Some agencies recommend that you take out insurance in the amount of £250,000 and upwards; again, you may want to discuss this with an accountant, or seek legal advice.

VAT registration can be done by yourself at no cost or through your accountant.

An excellent free guide to freelancing is available from the Professional Contractors Group (PCG) website. Go to **www.pcg.org. uk/cms** and you'll find everything you need to decide how to set yourself up and get started with the necessary admin for a freelance career.

SUMMARY

Consider the pros and cons of interim management by discussing them with someone who is working as an interim, or with an agent, or both. A course or seminar will help you decide. Then devise a CV that you think will sell your skills in the sector. Get feedback from an agent to determine if your CV will be effective.

When you start your first assignment, make sure that you have a contract and you have sorted out your admin requirements. When you're near completion, obtain a reference, update your CV, and look for your next assignment.

SUCCESS STORY:
GRAHAM STEPHENS

In 2000, following a long and successful career as Director of Customer Services in the IT sector, Graham Stephens saw a redundancy looming. He was able to negotiate a 'soft landing'; a good package that allowed him, at 50 years of age, to take a break and consider his options.

After a few months, a former employer called and asked him to take on a project as an interim manager. He enjoyed it so much that he decided not to accept a permanent role when it was offered. Instead he carried on working as an interim and, after three further assignments, he realised that what he liked best was setting things up and getting them running. With the permanent jobs he'd done, once clear goals had been established and a plan put into operation, his time was spent making sure things were ticking over – something that Graham found less stimulating. Interim roles meant that he faced a new challenge with every assignment. And it hasn't always been in IT; he's also worked for an oil and gas company and an image library.

After nine years, he decided that the long hours necessary in an interim role were not what he wanted in the next phase of his career. His interim experience has given him the opportunity to work in many different organisations, and he's now operating as a senior management consultant focused on leadership and management development. This is delivered through executive coaching and training. He often works in partnership with Southampton Solent University, where he was recently appointed to Visiting Fellow in the Faculty of Business, Sport and Enterprise. He is also starting to build his SME client base, which is all part of his plan to carry on working well into his 60s.

Graham has some sound advice for those getting started as an interim.

- Know what you're good at. You cannot be a jack of all trades.
- Understand the value that you can offer to companies.
- Make sure you are able to sell yourself as a *product*.
- Network like crazy and use LinkedIn. (All of Graham's interim work came through his own connections. In his case, he didn't find interim agencies very productive.)
- Get on the telephone and call people; there's no substitute for personal contact.

When you have the job, be prepared for surprises. Graham says that, even though a problem has been previously identified, you may find that the current management is part of the problem. Treasured systems that are still deemed to be effective by a company's founders might be the things that need to change. Political nous and diplomatic skills are very important in the role. Graham was once called in for an assignment by the chairman of a company, only to find that the MD did not want him there. Graham also cautions that being an interim is hard work and the hours are long; it's not for those who want an easy ride.

In his opinion, there is a gradual increase in the need for interims, with many businesses slow to recognise the benefits they can bring. He thinks that SMEs, in particular, could use interims and their expertise to catapult themselves to the next stage of growth.

CONSULTANCY 13

It sounds like an appealing situation: be your own boss, work as often as you like, sell your expertise for a high price and be recognised as an expert in your field. Others have been successful at it, so why not you?

The starting point is a rigorous assessment of your skills to determine that you have the essentials. Then you'll need to research your market, understand how to position yourself competitively and decide how to target customers and sell to them. If your skill set matches the profile of a consultant, you'll engage with two important questions: *'What is your proposition (what value do you bring your clients)?'* and *'Why should your clients buy your services when someone else might offer them cheaper and better?'*

THE BASIC REQUIREMENTS

There are two broad categories of essential skills: content and process. 'Content' skills include your specific technical knowledge. Do you have expertise that is rare or unusual, or which people and companies normally buy as required? For example: companies don't hire office managers as consultants but they might require a relocation expert to make recommendations on an office move. Lots of IT disciplines lend themselves to consulting because in-depth experience is needed for a short time. Business and management consultants are hired because they have specialist skills. The need for consultants can also be event-driven: the 2010 deep-sea oil rig leak in the Gulf of Mexico required people with highly specialised knowledge.

It isn't necessary to be unique or have an exotic specialism but it is important to:

- be credible with the depth of experience and knowledge in your field;
- be able to define specifically what you are offering;
- have something that companies or individuals want to buy.

To discover what 'content' skills you have, go back over your academic and work history and list the areas of knowledge that you know are highly developed. Make your list as thorough as possible. Look for situations where you analysed a problem and took action that resulted in measurable outcomes. Because you've had many years of experience in your field, you may have forgotten something that you haven't used recently but could be updated and made relevant. Try to be as inclusive and as specific as possible.

After that exercise, consider your 'process' skills. They fall into five categories:

1. *Problemsolving.* Also known in business schools as 'decision analysis', this is an essential skill for a consultant. You'll be expected to define the problem (or problems) and then work with your client to find solutions. It's important to be able to prove your problem-solving abilities to a potential client by using examples to show how you've influenced real-life situations. Be able to quantify the value: 'We *saved £10 million*' or 'We *grew the business by £150,000.*'

2. *Communication.* Many consultants consider this to be at least as important as their problem-solving skills. You'll have to be a good listener, be able to present well and write clear reports. If you're lacking in some of these abilities it may not be fatal; this is an area that can be improved by taking courses.

3. *Interpersonal.* Building relationships with clients, agents and other consultants is essential in order to obtain the contract and retain the client. Much of your future business will come from referrals. Your personality plays a key role here. Are you a person who gets on easily with others? Are you perceived to be someone who is credible and trustworthy?

4. **Marketing.** The ability to sell yourself and your business are key attributes. If you can't get customers you won't have a business. You will need to package and present yourself in a way that impresses clients.

5. **Business.** Even if you're gifted with technical and communication skills, you may not know how to run a business. A self-employed consultant needs to understand the basics of starting and operating a small business, which can be learned. Start with your local university or find seminars that are appropriate. See if you can meet with some consultants who are successful. Find someone with first-hand knowledge who will tell you what they have done to make their business run smoothly. Alternatively, you could form a partnership with someone who has that skill.

THE COMPETITION

As an occupation, consultancy has been around for a long time. There are many people who have been with large consultancy firms (such as KPMG and Deloitte), training and working for years and honing their craft. You'll be entering a highly competitive field, one that has been developed and cultivated by other experts. How will you position yourself?

You compete on the basis of your 'value proposition' in addition to your skills. If you take a good look at yourself and your market, you can determine if there are many other consultants out there in the same field. In terms of your speciality, if one person in ten has your knowledge, then you are less valuable than you would be if the ratio were one in a hundred or one in a thousand. Take some time to honestly assess your position with regard to others who are working as consultants in your field. Seek opinions from colleagues and friends. It's important to have a realistic view.

One way to overcome competition is to bring better value to clients. If you can convince them that you can do the same thing as a high-priced firm, then you could gain a contract. Being able to further illustrate the savings you will bring to the company will also aid your case. Will your work enable the client to make cost savings by improving systems or by increasing sales? Can you improve performance by bringing clarity to a contentious situation?

As you would in a job interview, you'll need to be prepared to show evidence based on your previous track record. You will be interviewed at some point in order acquire the contract, so if you find the process daunting it would be a good idea to get some professional coaching with someone who can assist you in preparing your pitch to clients. Your pitch will include several stories about your successful projects.

DEVELOPING YOUR PROPOSITION

Consider reasons that clients use consultants and then structure your offering to fit their needs. Consultants are hired in order to:

- provide expertise not available from within a company;
- supply objective advice from an outsider's perspective, someone removed from corporate politics;
- solve a problem that has no obvious solution; and
- improve performance in a specific area.

You may already have ideas to present to a company or a set of clients. In the course of your previous employment, have you identified inadequate systems that you know you can improve? Is there a sales channel that isn't being exploited? Are there personnel or recruitment problems in a firm? Can you present solutions?

This is an invitation to engage with entrepreneurial, outside-the-box thinking. Being able to imagine a solution is part of the consultant's remit. As an exercise, think of a company you've done business with (or worked for) and write down a solution to a problem that you've seen. Then think of a way to get in touch with a decision-maker at that company. Use your network and make a sketch of your route to that person. You may find that they're only one or two degrees of separation from you. If so, then there isn't much distance between you and your first client.

Contacting potential clients and sounding them out with your proposition will aid you in your decision to proceed as a consultant.

Your first clients will likely be people that you know in your industry. Read the success stories included in this chapter and you'll notice each consultant found clients in their network, and they continue to do so.

SUCCESS STORY: JANE EVANS

A career in HR led Jane Evans straight towards her own consultancy, with a move that was carefully planned and executed at the age of 45.

After taking a degree in Psychology at the University of Lancaster, Jane's first job was with Millward's Shoes, as a trainee in retail management. Then she joined the HR department at Mr Harry Frame Clothing, a move that she says was natural because of her psychology background and her interest in people. She left when one of their suppliers, Blue Arrow Personnel Services, offered her a job as a recruitment consultant. She was there for two years before she joined Vodafone to set up a recruitment function in the early days of the company's development. She stayed there for 18 years, always in HR, changing roles every two years and supporting a multitude of HR projects and activities, including mergers and acquisitions. In the year 2000, the company underwent a major restructuring, giving Jane an opportunity to develop her skills and expertise in organisation design, development and change, which subsequently became her speciality.

Jane left Vodafone in 2008, having progressed to a European organisational development role. She'd achieved the goals she had set herself within Vodafone and was looking for new challenges. Jane wanted to be master of her own destiny, with a better work-life balance, so she formed a consultancy partnership with a colleague from Vodafone. Jane says, 'We have a Venn diagram of skills that are complimentary and overlapping.' Their values are also in synch, something that is very important in their partnership. Integrity isn't compromised and clients know that they can be trusted; it's part of their brand.

Unlike other start-ups, these two found their clients relatively easily. Here's how they did it: first, they spent a lot of time on their value proposition. What exactly were they offering and why was it better? They developed a full understanding of what they were about before they made themselves available. Next, they developed a simple, attractive website. On the day the site went live, they contacted all of their colleagues and friends, directing them to the website by using a friendly tone that informed everyone they were ready to launch their business. That same day they got a response and an assignment. It sounds easy, but it should be noted that in their careers they had developed a fan base; not consciously, but simply through becoming known for the quality of their work and the effectiveness of their working relationships. Both of them had established sterling reputations and excellent connections in their field before they launched their business. They were very credible.

Here is Jane's advice for new consultants:

- Work out what makes you unique – most of the time it's simply the fact that you are you!
- Understand and be able to explain your value proposition, but be flexible to accommodate the client's real needs.
- Know who your proposition will appeal to, in what circumstances, and market to them appropriately.
- Have the right mental attitude about consulting.

Of course, there were many lessons learned along the way. Shortly after they started, and by way of testing out their offering, they presented their proposition to a 'friend of a friend' who was a well-known HR consultant. They were challenged hard about their presentation, with the recommendation that they find a way to explain why their offering was unique. After a rethink, they came up with an elevator pitch that captured what they were all about, without having to make a 10-slide presentation. Jane says it's important that your pitch is something you can use at any professional or social function, as well as with clients.

They don't try to compete with the larger consultancies, but seek clients whose culture and stage of development are more suited to their consultancy style. While at Vodafone, they had been regarded as 'internal consultants' who had to persuade their directors to work with them as an alternative to bringing in external consultants to do the work. This gave them an understanding of what clients are looking for, and what irks them about consultants too.

When asked what she would have done differently with the benefit of hindsight, Jane says, 'a lot more networking in my last year at Vodafone'. She readily admits that all of their clients come through their network. Jane has a few more words of advice.

- It is often more realistic to charge a day rate, rather than a project rate, as projects change and expand over time in unpredictable ways.
- Keep clients up to speed with changes that affect the budget. That way, there aren't any surprises.
- Sometimes it can be useful to showcase your work by offering some support to a client without expecting a fee – what goes around comes around.
- Maintain your portfolio of clients by keeping in touch and checking in on how things are going after you've left.

Finally, Jane says, 'Don't undersell yourself. Be confident that you're worth what you say you are worth.'

ROUTES TO CONSULTANCY

There are three ways to get started in consultancy.

1. ***Join a consulting company as a full-time employee.*** If you have specific expertise in an industry sector and lots of contacts, you may be an asset because you can develop new business for them. This approach builds career capital in the field. Freelance work remains an option for the future.
2. ***Become an associate.*** In this situation, you work on an as-and-when basis, taking projects that are assigned to you. This could be a good way to jump-start a consultant career because the selling and marketing are done by someone on your behalf. You get to be your own boss from day one, and still build up career capital as a consultant.
3. ***Become an independent/freelance.*** You're on your own: finding clients, getting contracts and delivering your services. This approach has the highest risk. When you're working on a project, you also need to be looking for your next client.

SUCCESS STORY:
NATALIE MCLELLAN

Natalie became a consultant with a career change that she made in her early 30s. She went freelance at the age of 40. It was a struggle at first, but she persevered and is now in a position to say that she thoroughly enjoys her work.

Natalie graduated in 1986 with a 2:1 in Modern Languages. She was hired by Cummins Engine Company in a corporate drive to recruit more women and, in her case, someone who had language experience to help them market to a variety of territories. She was assistant to the head of communications, doing publicity for OEM (Original Equipment Manufacturer) accounts. Then she had her first involvement with change, working as part of a director-level team, leading an initiative to deploy a customer satisfaction measurement programme and customer-led improvement process across the EMEA (Europe, Middle East and Africa) region. During her time at Cummins, she took an MBA, which was sponsored by the company. After ten years, a change in management at Cummins and a desire to broaden her experience meant that it was time to leave.

As a result of her MBA studies, Natalie was attracted by the idea of consultancy. She was able to join Ernst & Young as part of a mature hire scheme, and she spent two-and-a-half years there. Then she went to PricewaterhouseCoopers (PWC) as a principal consultant, leaving three years later as a director, after taking a voluntary redundancy. With children now on the scene, Natalie wanted to be self-employed and change her work-life balance. That was her primary motive for going freelance.

Her first attempt at a business start-up was not a success. The lessons she learned are worth noting. First, she spent 12 months working with a new partner who, like Natalie, didn't enjoy selling. So they spent 12 months polishing their proposition, instead of getting new business. Their offering was confusing to their customers: they were attempting to integrate branding, marketing and customer management. The proposition was difficult to sell to a client organisation. After much frustration – and a few contracts – she decided to go out on her own.

That wasn't as easy as she'd hoped: she spent ten months developing her relationships with agencies before she got her first contract in June 2005. And it was a step down in terms of the status she'd held previously, because it wasn't a full consultancy role. She worked for 11 months as a project manager (so she combined an interim role with consultancy) for an insurance company, helping them to define a new customer value proposition and associated operating model. Her next role was as strategic project manager with an international optician, where she put her strategy and business architecture knowledge (the core skills she acquired at PWC) to better use. As a consultant, she worked with the international director and the chief executive in evaluating the potential of a new business proposition. The insurance company brought her back in a customer relationship management role for a brief spell, and then she was hired by a private health insurer, consulting at board and senior management level. She was there for over two years, leading a variety of initiatives which included the establishment of a new business architecture capability and the definition of a new target operating model.

After five years operating as an independent consultant, she's come full circle and is undertaking the type of work she did with Ernst & Young and PWC. It hasn't been easy, but she is now able to land the kind of stimulating roles she enjoys and, at the same time, have the flexibility and control she needs as a working mother of three.

Natalie has a lot of useful advice for those who want to get started.

- Be patient. It was 10 months before Natalie got her first contract.
- Establish and maintain agency relationships. Her work at both insurance companies came through an agency.
- Pick one thing that you're really strong at and develop it further.
- Invest in yourself. Take courses (such as Project/Programme Management, Lean/Six Sigma) that enhance your skills and look good on your CV.
- Develop a massive network. Consultants need to know a lot of people, including interims and contract workers. Natalie has had work come to her though interims she has hired previously.
- Use LinkedIn.

Natalie says it's difficult to compete with a trained consultant such as herself, especially in a slow market, but people are doing it

> successfully. Developing a broad network of clients and agencies is key, as well as clearly defining the specialist expertise you offer to the market.

HOW NOT TO BE A CONSULTANT

Peter left his full-time job with the idea that his knowledge was valuable in his sector. In his opinion, finding clients wouldn't be a problem. He kept in touch with former colleagues, resulting in some consultancy work with his previous employer. He was happy to lose himself in a project for nine months, secure in the knowledge that he was being well-paid for his expertise. When the contract ended, Peter started looking for a new assignment. Time passed and the months rolled by until he realised he had to do something different because his business was failing.

What went wrong? First, he went straight to freelance without planning or preparation. Peter didn't develop a client base by networking and marketing himself. Next, he didn't consider how to develop himself as a product. Finally, he made the biggest error a business can make: he relied on one customer.

THERE IS A BETTER WAY

Start with a short-term contract with an ex-employer, but be sure to invest some of your earnings in workshops, seminars, and other activities that teach you to be an effective consultant. Build relationships with agencies that understand you and your field and hone your personal proposition. Develop your network and widen your contracts. Implement a system to generate a stream of leads. Consider becoming an associate with a consultancy firm. Create a marketing plan to sell your skills. Have plenty of leads to follow when your contract ends; one of them will get you your next client.

DEVELOPING YOUR BUSINESS FURTHER

Following a succession of contracts, you may be able to enter the second stage of a consultancy: taking on associates who will sell their time to companies, allowing you to earn a mark-up for yourself. To do that, you'll need to invest in your methods and systems, and also in marketing in order to attract associates as well as clients.

Good businesses develop long-term strategies. A formal business plan is a requirement, not only for your business, but also for your personal offering. A consultant needs to be up to date or their services will soon be obsolete.

MORE ABOUT THE BUSINESS

'Running your own business has three parts: fee earning, development and admin. The constant challenge is finding the right balance between the three.'
Paul Lower

If you've skipped the interim chapter and come straight here, be sure to go back and look at what we say about setting up as a limited company and the other admin requirements for a freelance business. As with interim work, a contract is essential. You can gain advice from an agency or from visiting the websites we recommend for freelancers. If your clients are individuals rather than companies, you may be able to initially operate as a sole trader, thus avoiding some of the paperwork that a company entails. Remember that companies do business with other companies, so you may not be able to attract corporate clients as a sole trader.

Try to charge a day rate for your services. Clients may want a fixed price for projects, but projects can change and expand (see Jane Evans' story on p.204). Price yourself competitively and know that you're worth what you're charging.

Nearly every sector has an association for consultants. Find the website for one that is relevant to you. Most of them have information about those working in the field, which agencies are active and recruiting, plus news and tips on how to get started and stay active. As well as helping you keep informed, joining an association will assist you in expanding your network.

SUMMARY

Analyse your 'content' and 'process' skills to determine if you have something to sell and if you will be able to operate effectively as a consultant. Research the market and see if there are customers for your offering. Develop your value proposition: be very clear about what you offer and the ways you can help your clients save money by improving sales, operations, or services. Be able to explain why you're worth what you charge. Test your proposition with an agency.

Once you're in business, invest time and money in personal development so that you stay current in your field. Always look for your next client while you're working on a project and, as we've said so many times before, network like crazy.

SUCCESS STORY: **PAUL LOWER**

Self-employment is a journey as well as a destination. Although Paul Lower set out to be a consultant – and he's had success as one – he discovered that what he really enjoys is an educator's role, training and coaching businesses of all shapes and sizes in his area of expertise: business finance. He came to this realisation when he discovered that his greatest satisfaction is in helping people understand what the numbers really mean, because numbers are the language of business. The message here is that you may not know what your best self-employed business will be until you get out and try something. Your efforts may lead you to unexpected places.

Paul has had an exciting career working in several different sectors. After leaving school in the early 70s, he started work as an accountant trainee at ASDA and left after three years as a partially qualified accountant. He landed a role at Heinz as a cost analyst while continuing his studies at night school for a full accreditation. His next job was at Coty (later bought by Colgate Palmolive) where he was Senior Management Accountant at the age of 24. In the late 70s he was recruited by Geosource, a US company, as

Regional Financial Controller. Their business was much different from the manufacturing background he was used to, in that they were involved in land-based geophysical exploration, primarily for oil. Paul was made Financial Controller for Africa, and his territory included Sudan, Nigeria, Somalia, Tanzania and what is now the Democratic Republic of the Congo. He left in 1983, with a full accountancy qualification and a desire to escape from an outbreak of cerebral malaria that was plaguing Africa at the time. A recruitment agency sent him to Polygram (now Universal Music) where he was made Senior Management Accountant at Phonogram, one of their subsidiaries. Those were high-growth times for the recorded music industry, as the 1980s saw most people replacing their vinyl records with high-priced CDs. Paul was asked to join Roger Ames in the creation of a new label: London Records. Ames was Managing Director and Paul was subsequently made Finance Director, a role he held from 1985–99, when London Records was sold to Warner in a deal that saw Ames become head of the worldwide interests of Warner Music. This meant a big change in corporate structure and, to an even greater extent, in corporate culture, so Paul took a redundancy package. David Hockman invited him to join Edel (a German record company) as Finance Director for a new music publishing division. Edel is famous for its rapid expansion and swift decline. An attempted management buyout did not succeed, his friend David left, and Paul continued to commute between the UK and Hamburg until he exited the company in 2002 – his second redundancy.

He decided to set himself up as a consultant in the music business. With his expertise and his contacts (two absolute prerequisites for a consultancy) he was soon working as a virtual finance director (two or three days a month, paid on invoice) for a music DVD company. He also developed an accounting software tool for Olswang, the media law firm, and a programme for the record business that incorporates advances, royalty rates and recording costs in one convenient package.

Music Sales, an international book and music publishing company, offered him a full-time job in 2004. He saw it as a challenge, taking a company that was organised on a federal basis and bringing it under central control. As Finance Director, a role he held for about four years, he replaced their accounting and reporting system and hired new staff to fit with the restructure. But the travel and long hours were taking their toll. In 2008, Paul had a rethink and decided to negotiate a withdrawal so he could be self-employed again. He didn't need a six-figure salary and he wanted to do work that was fun and engaging.

Now he offers business finance training and coaching. Drawing on his cross-sector experience, he can advise any type of business, from Angel Trains (a rolling-stock company) to Primark. His African connections have proved useful, and he's done work for the Nigerian public sector, helping their Civil Aviation Authority and Securities and Exchange Commission. He has also developed a course for one of the major Nigerian banks, teaching them to make improvements to their anti-fraud systems.

He knows that business training and coaching is a saturated market. How does he differentiate his business? He trains with the benefit of experience and he can research and develop bespoke courses. His one regret is that he named his company Paul Lower Consulting, because consulting is only a small part of his business.

SUCCESS STORY: **BEN MAKINS**

Once you have taken the decision to become self-employed you don't know where it will lead and things may not always turn out as planned. After many years as an employee in the public sector, Ben Makins became a consultant, started a new business with a colleague, was head-hunted to develop a consultancy within an established business and then joined a partnership. His story is an example of how to seize opportunities when they arise. And he has some advice for those public sector workers who might hope to emulate what he has done in the current market.

Ben graduated in the 1970s with a degree in Politics from York University. He acquired a professional qualification in social work and a Master of Social Work degree from York, followed by a Diploma in Management Studies from Coventry University.

He spent three years as a social worker with a rural team, working in the areas of mental health, child protection and older people's services. Then he moved 'from the dales of North Yorkshire to the wilds of Notting Hill', as he describes his relocation to London in the 1980s. Ben started as a senior practitioner in Kensington and Chelsea, before moving on to become a team manager and then area manager in Hounslow – a middle management position. In 1990, he faced his first redundancy at the age of 37 due to a restructure. Before the redundancy could occur, he successfully applied for a job at Ealing Council (effectively a promotion) and subsequently spent ten years there, first as an area manager and then in a number of roles – his final one as Assistant Director. In 1999, with a restructuring underway, Ben thought he would like to be self-employed. He used his previous experience of redundancy to negotiate an exit package that allowed him to stay in control and take some time to consider his options..

At the age of 46, he had a broad range of experience and a solid reputation. He got his first consultancy offer from his network That led to a second contract where Ben collaborated with a former colleague who had also gone freelance. They decided to team up and form their own service company, AQSC, which they managed for five years. They could have carried on, but his partner had different aspirations and didn't want to continue. Being head-hunted to develop and run a consultancy within Care and Health (a company with several interests) gave him the opportunity to refresh his networks. It was also a rich learning experience. However, after two years in the role he could see that, in spite of his own efforts, the company was going to fail. It was time to bail out. What to do?

Ben is an excellent networker, and so his problem was soon solved when he was approached by two former colleagues who invited him to join their limited liability partnership. Together they run SCP Consult, a service company that provides senior interim managers as well as consultancy and project management services to local authorities and primary care trusts. They work with over 100 associate freelances and have grown turnover five-fold in three years.

When asked if his approach could be replicated, Ben says it can't be done in the same way. The market is very different today than it was under 13 years of a Labour government, when there was growth in the number of service companies under contract to local and national governments. But while there is a backlash against big profits being earned from public services, there are still opportunities for small and medium firms with reasonable prices, which means smaller margins and low overheads. Some individuals will continue to work as consultants and interims but it won't suit everyone in the new environment.

Ben's advice to those wanting to be self-employed in the public sector is:

- get ahead of the game early;
- stay on top of a rapidly-changing landscape;
- don't rely on your title or station;
- analyse your skill sets and be able to show how you can think outside of your experience and comfort zone;
- be proactive and seek opportunities; focus on your experience and skills that would help organisations to innovate, make service efficiencies, cost savings, and performance improvements.

Ben says that in very lean times, smarter local authorities will take on people with strong skills to help them deal with making savings. For example: they'll be looking at procurement specialists who deliver results. He suggests having a good look at social enterprises such as mutuals or cooperatives as a way of providing services to councils, either by setting one up or acting as a consultant and advising clients as to how it should be done.

Ben has never regretted his decision to go out on his own. He admits that he could not have foreseen where it would lead, but the result has been a rewarding career.

START YOUR OWN BUSINESS

There's a new term that has been coined by the media, one that is also appearing on age-related websites: 'olderpreneur'. It's a play on the word entrepreneur, which is derived from the French *entreprendre*, meaning 'to undertake'. In most business cultures an entrepreneur is defined as someone who sets up a business that involves financial risk, and does so with the aim of making a profit. Typically, an entrepreneur will own and manage the business, either alone or in association with others, depending on the nature and size of the operation.

Our contacts at London Business Angels, a leading UK angel investment network, have told us that they are seeing an increase in the numbers of older entrepreneurs seeking funding. Age is a factor in reducing risk in a new venture and it is valued by some investors. Studies show that businesses started by olderpreneurs have a higher-than-average survival rate[1]. If the proposition and the team are sound, then business angels may be interested in investing. Angels are private individuals who invest in high-growth businesses in exchange for an equity share in a company. The fact that a company is managed by an older person can be a selling point, since trust is essential with angels. Evidence of capability builds trust.

The image of the entrepreneur as a flashy Richard Branson type is not wholly accurate. It takes courage to start a new business, and entrepreneurs are charismatic individuals, but success is achieved with a good idea and a great team. The lone entrepreneur is a myth. He or she depends on a partner or a small group that is central to the success of the operation. You may be one of those people: a valuable team member who, by working in combination with the right partners, will be part of a successful start-up. Alan Saxon (see p.228) is an example of someone who discovered that he was a valuable team member, someone essential to the success of a new venture.

TYPES OF ENTREPRENEURIAL VENTURES

Ownership, management, risk and profit are the basic components of an entrepreneurial venture. Corner shops, franchises and consultancies fit the definition, but they usually have one characteristic that differentiates them from companies that grow into big money-makers: they are 'lifestyle businesses'. If successful, they provide the owners with a good income that meets their needs and perhaps leaves something behind for the kids. You may decide that you want to start a lifestyle business. Matt Williams did, and he's happy with his choice (see p.220). There's plenty of information in this chapter for you to consider if you choose to create a lifestyle business – although we don't discuss franchises or buying a pre-existing business. Our expertise is with starting new businesses from scratch.

Funding for a lifestyle business often comes from the owner's resources, perhaps combined with a bank loan, credit line, or investment from relatives or friends. However, to attract funding from a third party, or a group outside of the owner's circle, a business must be 'scalable', which means it should have the potential for rapid growth and for generating future profit for the investors. In this chapter, we refer to a 'fundable business' as one that is scalable. That sets it apart from a lifestyle business that is entrepreneurial, but doesn't have the potential to grow to a size that can generate a big return on investment.

We'll look at the basic requirements of a business start-up in the light of what will attract investors – and business angels in particular – because if someone smart wants to own a share of your business, then you know you've got a better chance of success, whether you take the money or not. But if a lifestyle business is what you want, please read on as the tools and techniques described are equally relevant to any start-up.

SUCCESS STORY: MATT WILLIAMS

After being made redundant, Matt Williams decided that he would convert his experience into a business he could call his own. His pragmatic approach is a lesson in how to take the right steps in getting started.

Matt's first job was as an apprentice, working for his father's printing company. He left at age 29 as a deputy manager and spent 12 years with Field Packaging. He joined as a printer and worked his way up, first as a shift manager and then reaching the position of production planner. The company closed in 2000 and, after a brief stint in sales with Carter Litho, he was re-employed by his father's company in 2001 as production manager. When his father passed away in 2008, the corporate culture changed and Matt took voluntary redundancy and moved to a large firm in East London as production manager. He left after four months because the long commute from Maidenhead took all the pleasure out of his work. He found a position closer to home but that was soon ended by the recession. In 2009, Matt was 48 years old, unemployed and uncertain about his prospects as an employee in the printing business.

He considered that his options were as follows:

- get a job outside the industry;
- buy a printing company;
- buy a franchise;
- start a new business from scratch.

He quickly discounted the first choice. Printing had been his whole life; finding work in another sector was too daunting a task. As well as looking at the franchise option, he researched businesses that were for sale. His conclusion? Mortgaging his house to buy a standalone business, or perhaps a franchise for

£54,000, cost too much and had a lot of risk attached. Why not go it alone with a new venture?

Realising that he had a limited knowledge of how to run a small business, Matt enrolled in a course at Thames Valley University called Start Your Own Business. He learned the fundamentals and fleshed out his knowledge with a Business Link course: Foundation to Success. With new confidence and £8,000 of his own money, he set himself up in a digital printing business that he runs from home.

What's his unique selling point (USP)? Matt says he doesn't have one, but on further questioning he reveals that his customers come to him because he offers a friendly, personal service, unlike the online businesses that he is currently competing with. He's easy to deal with and he offers a very fast turnaround at a good price.

How does he get customers? Following instructions from his course instructors, Matt found that over 50 per cent of his business came through networking; he recommends 4Networking and Refer-on as two groups that are practical and useful.

He says that his biggest obstacle was overcoming the doubts and critical comments that were thrown at him by friends and other well-meaning people. He was strong and positive in his mind that this was what he really wanted to do.

At the moment Matt has a lifestyle business. He's doing something he enjoys, and he has a five-year-plan that may see him converting it into a scalable business by creating a franchise or developing a chain of printing shops. For Matt, this is just the beginning.

WHAT DOES IT TAKE?

You'll need six things to get started:

- a good idea;
- a great team;

- a market opportunity;
- growth potential;
- a sound business plan that describes all of the above;
- a business mentor.

It has to be said that energy, dedication and a love of business (or at least a love of the business you are starting) are essential. Without those qualities, you should be looking for another way to earn money. The road to success is long and arduous; passion for the enterprise is a basic requirement. It's better to start something you love doing, rather than creating a business you don't enjoy simply because you suspect it will make money. Utilise your talents and connections, and start locally – that's where your largest network is. Our two success stories in this chapter illustrate this point. Both Matt and Alan had lots of previous experience in their respective fields, and they genuinely like what they're doing.

1. The big idea

If you struggled in your former job with a product or service that wasn't fit for purpose and you think you can improve it, then you have an idea. If your nephew is a software programmer who's been bugging you to take a look at his latest program – one that makes something run faster and better – then you know someone who has an idea that you can develop into a business. In order to start a new venture it isn't necessary to invent something radical or earth-shattering; many successful businesses are built on improvements to existing products and services, or they take advantage of a 'dislocation' in the market, meaning a change in the way people do things. Mobile phones morphing into handheld computers is an example of a dislocation (think of the number of apps that Apple now has for its iPhone) or e-readers replacing books (whole new businesses have sprung up, such as digital warehouses for adapting and storing content and online bookstores that compete with Amazon by only selling downloadable books). As a general rule, it is easier to start a service business than it is to launch a product. That's because initial customers – an essential requirement – can be acquired through a simple and cost-effective manner by networking.

The best question to ask when evaluating a new business idea is: *Where's the pain?* Followed by: *How does my idea make the pain go away?* This strategy examines problems and solutions. The more painful the problem, the greater the value of the solution: your product or service. A cure for cancer would be extremely valuable, while a new way to get fresh vegetables to market would be lower down in a problem/ solution hierarchy.

How do you know if it's a good idea? If it survives a night at the pub with your friends and it appears to be sound in the cold light of day, that's a first step. But then you'll need to take it further by doing a lot of research to determine if your service idea is already in the market, or if someone is making and selling your gadget that beats all gadgets. Having convinced yourself that you might be on to something, the next thing is to run the idea past other people with expertise in your chosen field, preferably those whom you trust to be honest with you. Your idea must be credible beyond your circle of family and friends.

The best way to prove that an idea has merit is to find a customer. Your first sale, an order or a promise to buy, will confirm that you're on to something. So will an endorsement, either from your first customer or a respected person in your sector.

Earlier in the book, we mentioned the TMAY, or elevator pitch: a brief summary of who you are and what you're seeking. With an idea, a customer and an endorsement you can create a two-sentence elevator pitch that describes your business. The first sentence is the concept (the solution to a problem) and the second is the endorsement. So an example might be:

We've got a (insert product/service description) *for* (insert customer/ market description). *We've already sold to* (first customer), OR (name of notable person) *is supporting our concept.*

You can vary this according to your needs. It's a useful tool to help you describe your business without getting bogged down in technical language.

2. The core team

An idea isn't worth much unless it's well executed. Many investors believe that the team is the most important thing because, without excellent people managing a business, it has little chance of success. Your core team has to have what it takes to succeed, because in order to get funding you're going to have to sell your concept and your team to investors. They have to buy into what you're doing and, crucially, so do you. Team members don't have to know everything at first; willingness to learn and adapt are necessary attributes for everyone in a start-up. What's important is that key roles are filled by credible people.

The first person to consider is the 'lead entrepreneur': the man or woman who may have had the idea in the first place (but not necessarily). They will be the face of the company and the nominal boss. All of the core team will be equal but there must be a leader, someone to take the role of managing director. Without that person you will not appear credible in the market. Lead entrepreneurs have vision; they are confident, ambitious, energetic and driven. They're certain that the business is destined for massive success, and they're able to convince others that this could be true; they're brimming with energy and ideas about how to make it work. This is the person that investors examine closely. They need to see two qualities above all others: enthusiasm and trustworthiness. And when it comes to trust, older entrepreneurs can have an advantage.

There is sometimes a dark side to the lead entrepreneur: they can be arrogant and manipulative, and prone to dishonesty when stressed. When building a team, look for those who can temper the worst traits, and always include process-oriented people to manage the details – an area where most lead entrepreneurs are often woefully inadequate.

Your core team must include a member with sales experience. A start-up without a sales person has no hope of success. That's because every business is all about cash flow. Someone has to make the deals and close them; no sales means no cash, which means no business. This is the team member who gets your all-important first customer (if the lead entrepreneur hasn't already), the one who can make cold calls, the one who has a list of contacts and a multitude of potential leads, or at least the talent and enthusiasm to get them. Some would argue that a marketing professional is what's required; that's only a good idea if your marketing person can also sell. Selling means closing and marketers aren't always very good at that. You can outsource marketing services and bring on a full-time person later. What you need is sales.

There will be a technical person on the team, the brains behind the product or service. In a creative business, this could be the designer, author or filmmaker; in IT the programmer fits the bill; pharmaceuticals will have a scientist. Many businesses have engineers in this role. A delivery specialist is also required: someone to make sure the thing gets made and into the shops, or that the techies show up and repair the equipment as specified.

A start-up is more credible to investors when there is a finance director (FD) on board. Funders want to know that their money is in safe hands and it's being used properly. They will expect timely and accurate reporting. Regular cash-flow forecasts are required and they should be created by a dispassionate team member, one who won't overestimate a potential income stream. This is the person who can sort out the admin. Even without any initial outside investors, all the other team members will be much happier if they don't have to deal with the bank or the tax inspector. Accountants are required for this role, not bookkeepers, who can be hired by the finance person on a part-time basis. You can have a part-time finance director. A small business doesn't require a full-time person in this role, especially at the outset. If your idea is good enough, you can attract a qualified accountant to act as FD by offering shares for their labour. Between five and ten per cent is usual, and with no salary on offer until a pre-agreed point. This type of FD is trading skills for equity and, for small operations, this is an excellent arrangement.

A core team could be structured like this:

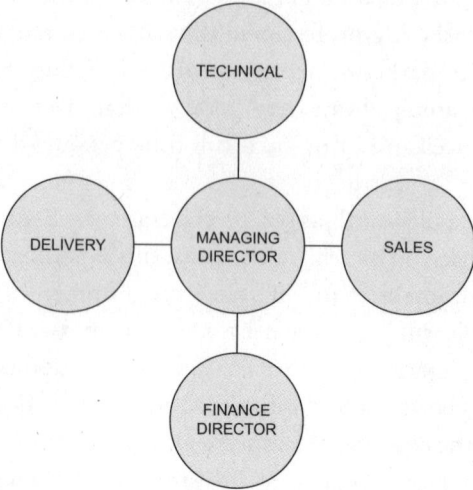

Fig. 14.1 Core Team

The team represented above is an example. There is no absolute requirement in having five people. However, the *roles* described need to be filled. It's possible for team members to combine roles, as long as there is an MD and three basic functions are covered: sales, finance and production/delivery.

A smaller core team might look like this:

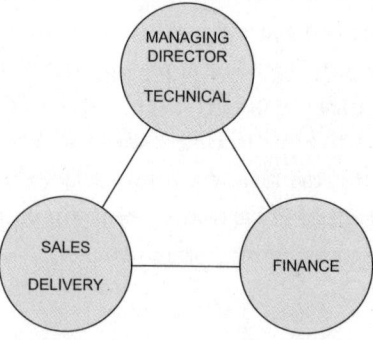

Fig. 14.2 Smaller Core Team

It's best for a start-up to have an odd number of principals. Even numbers don't work as effectively because start-ups need to be light on their feet, able to seize opportunities and act on them quickly; majority decisions are required. Getting bogged down in a two-against-two deadlock is counterproductive and very common in a company of four.

Will a start-up work with two people? Many successful companies had only two core members at the beginning: Apple and Google, for example. However, an FD should be added to the mix (as above) and then you're back to the number three if you've given the FD voting power, which they must have on decisions of a financial nature.

It's best if everyone in the core team is an equal shareholder (except your part-time FD, if that is your arrangement). The team must be incentivised, free to work hard without feeling that they're helping someone else get rich, especially since most of the members will not be drawing a realistic salary at first. The lead entrepreneur/MD might object if it was their idea, but they should be persuaded that a company of equals is a company that's much more likely to succeed. Everyone's equity will be diluted if the business can attract investment – that's the nature of the game. However, by retaining equal status with each other before and after funding, all of the principals will keep their dignity and passion for the long journey to success. Consider that everyone in the core team will be a future board member and successful companies have strong boards.

Choose reliable people for your team, those whom you trust and respect, with talents that are complementary to yours. You'll have to like them too, because you'll be spending a lot of time together. Family members and close friends are usually not a good idea if you value the long-term relationship. Businesses do fail, even those that are strong at the outset, and you won't want to lose a marriage or a friend if it all goes wrong.

SUCCESS STORY: **ALAN SAXON**

One way of staying active and credible in your sector is by taking short-term contracts. Instead of waiting for the perfect job, Alan Saxon decided to create opportunities that might pay off in future. The result was an offer to join a new venture as a valued team member; now he's an entrepreneur.

Alan's experience in packaging is extensive. He left his first job with a printing company after eight years, having risen to the position of senior designer, with clients that included Boots and Marks & Spencer. He was hired by a major toy company, Kenner Parker Tonka, where he was European Package Development Manager for ten years. (Those who remember the original *Star Wars* merchandise will have seen samples of Alan's work.) He was happy there, and would have stayed had the company not entered Chapter 11 bankruptcy protection in the US, resulting in a corporate sale to Hasbro in 1989. The new operation had no packaging development department, they used different working methods and so Alan found himself sidelined. He left for a position at Woolworth's where he stayed for 17 years, until the demise of the company in 2008. Deloitte was the receiver. They rang Alan because he knew where many of the brand assets were located. That got him a three-month contract with Argos, helping them with one of the brands they had purchased, and he began his search for a full-time position.

Alan discovered that ageism would play a big part in his struggle for re-employment. He was 58 years old, something that was easy to detect from his CV because he put down the dates of his education (not necessary) and he listed his first job, which confirmed that he was older. He says that he didn't know how to write a tactical CV, i.e. one that's written to target a job ad (rather than a full chronological history) and he's certain that meant lost opportunities. After a couple of sessions at the Job Club, he rectified the situation but continued to have trouble finding a permanent role. Alan applied for jobs that were tailor-made; some of them matched his job description at Woolworth's. He knows he was passed by in favour of younger workers and he doesn't understand why employers wouldn't hire him.

His solution was to take contracts for a limited term and work for much less than his former rate, in the hope that a better job would emerge through the contacts he made. He was approached by a small design studio in London and worked there for three months, developing pitches for some big brands. His only remuneration was his expenses. Following that, he used his network to land another short (but paid) contract with a company that wanted to expand into multilingual packaging, one of his areas of expertise. He proved his worth and, even though the company didn't survive, the owner asked Alan to join him in a new venture: a start-up.

The company is a language service provider, supplying translations and branding. They believe they can take on the big agencies by offering a high-quality, lower-cost alternative in a market where price is an issue. They're a small outfit with eight employees, and Alan was offered a senior role as Head of Operations, with equity shares in the company. He accepted the offer. Prior to this, he'd never considered himself an entrepreneur, but he is now a member of the core team – he's their delivery expert. The MD considers him to be his right-hand man. Alan believes in the other team members; together they're set to grab a share of the market.

Alan's looking forward to taking this as far as he can. 'It's invigorating to try new things,' he says, 'and it's a chance to see what you're made of.' He's 59 and he sees a bright future for himself and his new company.

3. The market opportunity

Your product or service must have an obvious differentiation in the marketplace, or there is no opportunity. What makes it special? What makes it stand out from your competitors? What is the USP? The strength of your USP will determine your position in the market and the size of the opportunity.

Answer the questions below to better understand your USP and your business:

- Who will buy this product/service?
- Why will they buy it?
- How many/how often will they buy?
- Why would they buy more over time?
- Why would they buy it from your company?
- What value are you actually delivering to your customers?

To attract funding, you'll have to demonstrate that there is a genuine opportunity and then be prepared to explain why your product or service will succeed in the market. It is essential to answer these questions for lifestyle businesses, as well.

4. Growth potential

Stand outside of your business and look at it like an investor. Focus your mind on the scale of your enterprise and imagine you are selling the business in five to seven years. What will it be worth? A person who invests £100,000 for 20 per cent of the company expects to get a return of a million pounds – ten times their original investment – on their share of the company at the time of sale. That's the rate of return angel investors are seeking. They may not get it, but they need to believe that it's realistic and possible.

So what will the business be worth in order to return a million pounds to someone with a 20 per cent share? The company value, at sale, would be five million pounds. What will turnover be at the time of sale? How can you grow your business to that size? What steps will you take to reach that goal? These are all questions that relate to scalability. You will need plausible answers before you seek investment.

Keep in mind that funders don't invest in lifestyle businesses – it's one of the biggest turn-offs. So if your chip shop can't become a best-selling chain of chip shops, then you should be content with a small operation. And there is nothing wrong with that, if it is your goal.

5. The business plan

You can start your business without a business plan, but that would be like hiking in new terrain with no map. Your plan won't be etched in stone; it will change over time, as you identify and face new challenges and opportunities, but it is essential to have one right from the start. You will have written project and business plans as a manager or professional, so this won't be the onerous task that frightens some younger entrepreneurs.

Think of your business plan as a story: one that explains where you are now, where you want to go, the people you're travelling with, and why those people are the best ones to take on your voyage. Tell investors why they should help to fund the ship and the crew. They need to know about the wonderful lands of profit that are your destination. You'll also have to tell them about the reefs and shoals you will encounter, how you plan to sail around them, and how you're rigged for stormy weather.

The sections of a business plan are typically as follows.

- Executive Summary (1–2 pages).
- Management Team: qualifications and experience.
- Product or Services: description and necessity (2 pages).
- The Market: detailed research, customers and competitors (3–4 pages).
- Operational Details: facilities, premises and suppliers.
- Strategic Planning: sales and marketing (2–3 pages).
- Financial: equity distribution, cash-flow projections (2–3 pages).
- Appendices: as required, and include a diagram of milestones.

The plan needn't be 50 pages long; something between 15 and 20 pages will be sufficient at the outset. You're writing for the average person, so use plain English and make it as free from technical jargon as possible. The Executive Summary must be at the front, with appendices at the back, but otherwise the order as outlined above can be varied.

If you're seeking funding, include an exit strategy for your investors in the financial section. Don't worry about how that will come about – it will either be a trade sale or an IPO (initial public offering of shares); the nature of your business will determine which one. It's the company valuation at sale that's difficult to predict, but your FD or a valuation expert can help you make an educated guess.

Once you have written your complete plan, go back and spend time on the Executive Summary, the first document that someone will ask for before they read the rest of your plan – rather like the covering letter that stimulates interest in a CV. The summary will clearly state the opportunity and the product, where you are now, what your vision is for the future, who is in the company, how you plan to achieve your vision and how long it will take to get there. The body of the plan is where you provide evidence to support the statements that you've made in your Executive Summary.

There are plenty of good books to help you write your plan and one, in particular, is mentioned in the Resources section which starts on page 253.

6. Mentors

Even with experience in your field, there will be holes in your knowledge: unforeseen hazards, potential customers and additional sources of revenue you may not be aware of, or competitors who might finish you off before you get started. Contacts outside of your team with experience of your business can provide invaluable guidance through the troubled waters of your start-up. You might find a mentor at your professional association, or perhaps through your network. Try to get one (or more) as soon as you can. A mentor can be of enormous help to a new venture.

MORE BASICS

Concurrent with the six things you need to get started (as above) there are several other tasks that need to be completed:

- choose an appropriate name;
- acquire a web domain (URL);
- incorporate as a limited company;
- draft and sign a shareholders' agreement;
- register your trademark;
- get patents for formulas and designs;
- find premises.

Some companies have websites that make name searches and incorporation very simple. They also provide information on the different responsibilities that companies and company directors undertake. You should make yourself familiar with those responsibilities before you incorporate as a limited company. Having a web domain is essential and it's easy to get one. See the Resources section for a short list of websites that will help you get started with the basics, including trademark and patent registration.

A word on registering your trademark: try to register the company name (or trading name) as your trademark. It can be done, and that way you won't have to worry about registering your logo as a trademark. Your logo may change over time, and this way you retain rights to incorporate your name into any logo as you see fit. Also register your company in as many categories of trade as possible, thus allowing for future business possibilities.

Premises are necessary for your start-up. That's because there is a perception that sole traders work from home. It's also best for your budding enterprise to have a base where the core team can meet regularly, as well as for conducting business in professional surroundings. A word of caution: make it as simple and cheap as you can. There's no need for an expensive office at first, unless you're starting a luxury brand and your customers need to see you residing in splendour. A few desks, a phone line, and Internet access are usually sufficient.

A shareholders' agreement is often overlooked by many start-ups, and that can cause problems later. On incorporation, your company will have drawn up articles of association that describe the relationships between shareholders and directors. Together with the memorandum of association, these documents comprise the constitution of the company, which sets out the internal legal framework. However, there a number things that are often not covered. What if a shareholder dies? What if one of the directors fails to perform as agreed? Should that person retain all of their shares while the other directors do the work? These matters can be covered by a shareholders' agreement: a private, legal letter that can specify any number of things including provisions for dispute resolution, agreements regarding the sale and disposal of shares, disbursement of salaries and dividends; and the appointment and removal of directors. Think of it as a prenuptial agreement that you make before you marry your business partners. Having one in place will not only put your mind at ease, it will also enable potential investors to understand your corporate governance. Upon investment, your investors will become new shareholders, and they will insist on drafting a new shareholders' agreement, subject to negotiation. Be sure to seek professional advice on all legal matters pertaining to your company.

FUNDING

The best way to run a business is by using the 'lemonade-stand' method. You purchase the ingredients with your own money, sell the lemonade at a price that covers costs (including wages) and earns a profit, and then you retain some of the profit and use the rest of it to invest in more lemonade stands until you've got dominance in the local lemonade-stand market, and so forth. It's also called the 'organic' method, which refers to the absence of funding, not the lemons. If you and your team can do this you'll be happier in the long run. Your net returns to the initial shareholders will be higher because you won't be sharing equity with investors, and you won't have a bank loan to worry about. If you never need outside investors and your business grows to a massive size, you'll have accomplished a truly great thing. It's an ideal that many businesses can't achieve, especially if capital costs are high at start-up, or the company requires development funding at any stage. There will come a time, hopefully later rather than sooner, when you will need outside investment to grow the business. Funding sources are listed below.

1. 'Soft' money: yours, family and friends. Money that doesn't come with hard terms of repayment, or require an exchange for equity.
2. Grants.
3. Bank loans, including those under the Enterprise Finance Guarantee scheme (formerly known as the Small Firms Loan Guarantee scheme, or SFLG for short).
4. A line of credit.
5. Strategic money.
6. Business angels.
7. Venture capital funds (VCs).

Loans or overdrafts are only good if you know you can repay them. They are favoured by some because it means you don't have to give up equity. However, if your cash flow is uncertain, or you are asked to put your house up against the loan or credit line (which is likely) then angel investment can be a better choice.

Strategic money is acquired when a customer pays in advance in exchange for an option on future rights. That means that a small share of equity is sold to the customer at an agreed date. It's smarter to get your customer to pay in advance without giving up equity, if you can.

As mentioned previously, business angels are private individuals who typically invest from £100,000 to £1 million in a new venture. They do this in exchange for a negotiable equity share in the company. Angels are a good solution for most new businesses that aren't well-funded at the outset, or when there is an increased capital requirement for growth at an early stage. Why? Because unlike a bank loan, you don't have to pay them back and, if you are fortunate or choose wisely, they will bring valuable business expertise to your operation. In exchange for which you will relinquish a percentage of equity in your company.

There are an estimated 18,000 angel investors in the UK, investing between £800 million and £1 billion in SMEs per year[2]. Approximately nine in ten are male and over the age of 50. Many will have an entrepreneurial background; some will be semi-retired or have retired from a successful business career (for an example of a business angel, see William Priest's story p.243). An angel will typically invest between 10 and 20 per cent of their wealth in a number of different ventures. In order to be part of an angel network they will have to certify as a high net worth individual, earning over £100,000 per year or having net assets of over £250,000, those assets *not* being a primary residence *or* including insurance contracts and pension benefits. They can also join a network if they meet the requirements of a self-certified sophisticated angel investor.

Your Uncle Robert can act as an angel to your business if you can persuade him to part with his hard-earned cash. However, as a family member, there could be hard feelings if things go wrong. An angel from a network will dust himself off and move on to the next exciting venture.

Angels invest for a number of reasons. It's often a way of staying involved in a sector they understand. There is tax relief under the Enterprise Investment Scheme (EIS) and your company will need to qualify[3]. Angels put in high-risk money, so it's a form of gambling – but a sensible angel will never bet more than he can lose. He will often invest in a company as part of a syndicate with a lead investor; many angels will put in amounts from £10,000 to £25,000 in several different ventures. As we mentioned above, angels expect a return of ten times their initial investment, generally after a three to five-year period. The expected rate of return is high because they anticipate losing money on four in five of their investments. If a single one earns as predicted, it pays for the losses *and* puts the angel in a profit position.

You can find angels by looking at the website for the angel network trade body, the British Business Angels Association. There you will find a list of angel organisations in your region. Angels invest close to home: about one hour's travel or within 100km from their place of residence. They want to be able to visit you at the office, but usually not to pester you. You should choose your angels carefully, and do as much diligence with them as they will with you. Every angel organisation has regular presentation evenings, where companies pitch to qualified investors. You'll receive the information you need to prepare yourself when you make your enquiry.

Given that most angels are over 50 and they like to invest in a sector they understand, you will usually encounter angels who know what you are doing. Remember that evidence of credibility builds trust, and as an older person your business experience can mean that you and your proposition are more plausible. Trust is very important to an angel, so if you can convey your enthusiasm and present a sound plan, you're more than halfway there.

Venture capitalists (VCs) are last on our list of funding sources because they do not usually invest amounts under £2 million, their equity demands are onerous, and they always insist on a fast-growth strategy that puts huge pressure on companies. Unless your business has a very large capital requirement at start-up and no foreseeable revenue stream until later in development, there is no need to share your business with VCs at an early stage.

CHALLENGES FOR 'OLDERPRENEURS'

We would be remiss if we didn't point out some of the difficulties, aside from risk, that are faced by olderpreneurs. The following list is based on one issued by the Silver Academy[4], a partnership between South East Chambers and the University of Surrey.

1. *Personal sacrifice.* It is hard work and the hours are long. There will be an impact on your family. Some new businesses (see Ben Makins' story, page 215) are less demanding in that the owners can create income without a large capital investment and adapt their hours to suit the demands of the business. Not all businesses are like that.

2. *Financial insecurity*. This can be stressful for many people. An uncertain income won't suit everyone.
3. *Loss of company perks.* Start-ups can't afford benefits like pensions and paid holidays.
4. *Isolation.* Being your own boss, or part of a very small team, can be lonely. A network of helpful contacts will ameliorate the situation.

BUSINESS ADVICE

Try to fill in the holes in your knowledge before you get started. Visit the Business Link website for general information: **www.businesslink. gov.uk**. PRIME is an initiative started by the Prince of Wales to assist over-50s in starting their own business. They have an excellent website: **www.primeinitiative.co.uk**. Your local council, college or university may offer courses or know where they are located.

SUMMARY

If you have a good idea – one that you're passionate about – you know you have customers for your product or service, you fit the description of a team member, and you can build a team to drive your business forward, then you may be ready to start your own business.

Most of the attributes that funders seek are the same ones that every business needs. If you're happy to stay small and have a lifestyle business, be aware that outside investors won't be interested. You'll need a scalable business to attract funding.

Seek as much advice as you can beforehand and be sure to find a mentor. As well as customers, your success will depend on having as many positive supporters as you can muster.

PORTFOLIO CAREER

CHAPTER 15

Over time, you've developed a variety of interests and talents. Arriving at a crossroads in middle age can be an opportunity to utilise them and create income streams from several sources. If you do that, you'll have a portfolio career. It might consist of two or more part-time jobs, or it could be a combination of work activities that includes regular wages combined with self-employed earnings from freelance and consulting work, a small business you've set up, or teaching. Any combination would qualify you as a portfolio worker; the key point is that you are doing more than one job simultaneously (in any given week or month), rather than sequentially (one contract following another).

There was a time when this type of career lacked respectability and someone who practised it was called a jack of all trades, perhaps with a tone of derision. That has changed in the past two decades as jobs for life have disappeared and the concept of permanent employment has been replaced with more flexible attitudes towards work. If you decide that this is the route to take, you may also have to adjust your personal thoughts about employment.

'To have a portfolio life you need to think beyond simply having or not having a job.'[1]
Dr Barrie Hopson

The term 'portfolio career' was coined in 1989 by management guru Charles Handy. In his book *The Age of Unreason*[2], he describes a 'portfolio worker' as someone who holds a number of jobs, clients and types of work all at the same time. Handy's five portfolio categories were defined as:

1. wage work: earned as an employee;
2. fee work: payment for results delivered;
3. study work;
4. gift work: for charities, friends or in the community;
5. home work: care of the home and family.

Adrian Bourne, co-author of *Building a Portfolio Career*[3], adds another category: 'Time for you', meaning holidays and non-work pastimes. He says the portfolio concept involves ring-fencing time for all of life's activities.

You may already have an unpaid work portfolio that includes numbers 3, 4 and 5 above. We'll discuss creating a paid work portfolio, combining items 1 and 2, perhaps with additional earnings from a small business you might have. The exciting thing about a portfolio career is that you decide what the balance will be; your work life will not be controlled by a single employer.

Charles Handy practises what he has preached. He resigned his full-time professorship at London Business School to create a 'portfolio life'[4]. For him that means an annual work-life balance where 100 days are spent earning money, 100 days are set aside for writing, 50 days for what he considers 'good works', and 100 days are for spending time with his wife, photographer Elizabeth Handy, with whom he has co-authored several illustrated books.

FOUR TYPES OF CAREER PATHS

To understand the portfolio concept better, it helps to have a look at different career types and compare them with what you have done in your working life. Four categories are defined by Barrie Hopson and Katie Ledger in their book *And What Do You Do?: 10 Steps to Creating a Portfolio Career*[5].

1. Single track: one career

By this, we mean a career as a doctor, lawyer, engineer, or teacher (as examples). This is considered a traditional career, where the end point is retirement at the end of a long climb upwards on the career ladder.

It used to mean job security (which isn't necessarily so any more), a pension and the identity that comes with a job title. In one or two words you can describe yourself to another person. This path is the one that most mature workers have been following. Vocational counsellors told us what we were best suited for, we got qualifications and then we specialised in a particular sector, looking for opportunities to move upwards.

If you've been in a single-track career, it may be difficult to imagine yourself doing anything else or having the time to develop a new work interest. But it's a bit like having a one-track mind: if you see only one thing as possible, then other options don't become apparent.

2. Serial career

Here you can move up, down, or sideways as on a chequerboard, changing sectors – or areas within a sector – every few years. Essentially, it means following your interests. People who do this are motivated by a desire to develop new skills and acquire fresh knowledge; they seek challenges that aren't available in a single-track career. The downside to this approach is that a serial CV may be hard for employers to understand, and people who do this can be regarded as flighty, even though they dedicate themselves completely to any work they undertake.

For an example of a person who followed a serial career path, read William Priest's story on p.243. William has worked as a civil engineer, a management consultant and as a senior vice president in telecoms. Each time he made a change he was pursuing an opportunity that was personally challenging.

3. Lifestyle career

People who do this are adapting their work to the way they like to live, instead of the other way around. If you know someone who works part-time in order to bring up children, or takes an undemanding job so that they can pursue a hobby that doesn't offer financial reward, you've met someone with a lifestyle career. They may not be rich, but it's quite possible they're happy.

4. Portfolio career

The simplest definition is 'someone who has two or more jobs with different employers, one of whom may be yourself'[6]. The jobs may be unrelated, or they may be similar, as in William Priest's portfolio. This is not a substitute for the first three career paths, nor is it having a group of unsatisfactory part-time jobs. It's a strategic way to achieve financial and personal goals.

MOVING TOWARDS A FLEXIBLE WORKFORCE

We've included the definitions above to illustrate that there are options besides the single-track career that many older workers will have pursued. In postwar Britain – as in the rest of the Western world – a single-track career has been the cultural norm. Schools educated future workers to find a single occupation at an early age; agencies, recruiters and coaches guided and encouraged the practice (they still do) because corporate hiring policies demanded it. There hasn't been much room for the Renaissance man, a multi-talented character resigned to history (although nowadays we might call such a person a polymath). Our economy demanded specialisation. It still does, but there is good evidence that things are changing. Corporations are now asking for a flexible workforce; they're looking for people who can bring special skills to short-term projects. Portfolio workers can do that.

It's possible to move between career types. Starting a portfolio career doesn't necessarily exclude you from returning to a single-track or serial career, but it has become a respectable option. The trend began with older workers and is now growing throughout all generations. Bourne says, 'The decline of the old contracts of certainty between employer and employee has led people of all ages to seek a life of careers, not a career for life.'[7]

SUCCESS STORY: **WILLIAM PRIEST**

A portfolio career offers freedom and variety, something that isn't usually available in mainstream, full-time employment. William Priest decided it was his most appealing career choice, because it means he can pursue several interests simultaneously and stay involved with business ventures he is passionate about. William has worked at a senior level in several sectors, gaining experience and developing a personal business strategy that has served him well. He's now applying that strategy to his portfolio career.

His BSc in Civil Engineering, followed by an MSc in Water Engineering, led him to work on agricultural development projects in Africa, at the age of 22. He says he was given the opportunity to manage big projects as a young man (some were funded by the World Bank) because he was prepared to take a risk and work in Africa. He had eight years' experience as a civil engineer when he decided to make a major career change. With a young family to support, overseas assignments were no longer suitable and he wanted to earn more. He chose management consultancy and then spent eight years in the sector, working for PA Consulting Group, Ernst & Young, Unisource NV and Price Waterhouse, where he left as a senior manager when he was offered a job by a client in the telecoms sector. It was a sideways move and one that he made because he was more interested in tackling a new challenge than climbing the career ladder.

William spent three years working for IBM Global Services, growing their European telecoms business. His next move was to take a small step down on the career ladder, a strategic decision that saw him getting promoted much faster than his contemporaries. He started as UK Director of Professional Services at Equant (the global B2B network service provider majority-owned by France Telecom) and finished as Senior Vice President at Orange Business Services (wholly owned by France

Telecom from mid-2005) where he was Head of Global Strategy, Marketing and Communications. How did he do it? During his first year at Equant, he exceeded his performance targets. That got him noticed by an influential board member, someone who was able to help him attain a board position by 2004. He stayed for a further three years and then decided to manage his way out; that gave him the time and money to consider a change.

William chose to spend six months considering his next career move. He spoke to many different search firms and companies – from consultancies to corporates – before joining Airwaves Solutions as Executive Director for Strategy & Marketing. The company was going through a transition and change that led to a major restructuring to focus on core offers and markets. This led to a smaller company and less potential for William to achieve what he wanted, so he saw that it was a good time to re-evaluate his options.

Was a CEO role the next best career move or a more varied and plural career after nearly 30 years of corporate life? Having built up a number of non-executive board roles over the previous couple of years, William felt it was a good time to become more involved with these smaller, entrepreneurial companies. He decided to leave Airwave and embark on a portfolio-based career. He now spreads his time between five organisations – four in the private sector and one large public sector board role. This enables him to bring the experience he has gained in the past to add value to these businesses and it allows him to continue to learn and develop. At the age of 52, he still believes in personal development and growth.

Here's a list of what his portfolio contains:

- **Non-executive Director at WorldSkills London 2011. He advises on marketing, branding and strategy.**

- Board Advisor, investor and Non-executive Director at Intergence Systems Ltd.
- Angel investor in two companies. As well as investing, he is a Non-executive Director.
- Executive Board Director at IP Innovation Partnerships Ltd. The partnership raises funds and invests in start-up businesses and assists them in accelerating sales growth.

It's easy to see from this brief précis that William is an ambitious and self-motivated person (he is someone who moves towards a goal, rather than away from a consequence – see Chapter 2). His drivers have always been challenge combined with opportunity. Staying in the same organisation or sector for a lifetime wasn't as important to him as taking a risk and being rewarded by success in a new endeavour. His career strategy was to keep learning, find new opportunities and embrace risk when it's balanced with common sense. He saw his situation as a mid-life opportunity. Instead of seeking a return to corporate life and the daily grind it entails, he chose to pursue a portfolio career, and he planned for it while he was in his last full-time position. Note that there is an obvious synergy in his activities, given that much of his time is spent in helping new enterprises get up and running.

For those who are considering a portfolio folio career he has the following advice:

- plan for your portfolio while you are in full-time employment;
- use your networks;
- join executive network forums;
- look for opportunities that interest you;
- try things outside of your comfort zone.

Now that William has embarked on a portfolio career his business life is under his control – and it is more creative – something that wouldn't be possible if he was director of a large company. It also gives him the option of returning to South Africa in the coming years. After all this time, William still has a heart for the region, and he'd like to return in some capacity to work or to support development activities.

IS IT FOR YOU?

Those with multiple skill sets and a wide range of interests and who have little trouble 'changing hats' in the middle of the day or week are suited to a portfolio career. If you're in doubt, answer the following questions:

- Are you self-directed and self-disciplined?
- Are you prepared to take risks?
- Does the idea of working on several different projects excite you?
- Can you handle pressure?
- Are you flexible in your thinking *and* in your work routines?
- Do you like new challenges?
- Would you rather take a low-paying job you enjoy rather than one you dislike, but which pays more?
- Have you got the financial flexibility to manage your life with a variable income?

You don't have to answer 'yes' to each one, but if most of your responses are affirmative, you can move forward with some confidence.

WHEN TO START PLANNING

Ideally, you start to plan your portfolio while you are in employment. But if you have been made redundant and this is the first time you've considered this option, don't worry. In the case of older workers, most portfolio careers come about as a result of a redundancy. For many, a portfolio career is what happens, not what is planned. A part-time job could lead to a private contract, a voluntary role becomes a paid one, then another job is bolted on, until it's obvious that a portfolio exists.

GETTING STARTED

It's best to be proactive and plan your portfolio career. Once again, it's time to get out paper and pen. You're going to imagine a new life for yourself. Note that this is similar to the exercises that you did in Chapter 5, which were aimed at creating a singular goal and a strategy to support it. In this case, there is a plurality of options for you to consider.

Use your self-assessment from Chapter 4 to find your list of motivated skills. These are the abilities you get up in the morning to use – your life would be boring if you didn't. They are your key to creating a successful portfolio. The concept here is to play to your strengths; there's no point in starting new work based on skills that you've had to develop later in life to overcome a deficiency. You may have to use those skills when you undertake a job in your portfolio, but the important thing is to base your portfolio career on motivated skills: the ones you use with enthusiasm, the ones that feed your passion.

Stand back from your list and consider jobs where those skills are used, jobs that may be done on a part-time basis – not one permanent full-time job. You're thinking about teaching a swimming class, not running the pool. Or perhaps you could offer accountancy services to small businesses rather than a major corporation. If top-level management is your passion, you could follow William's example and take on several non-executive director roles.

Now make another list: one that is dedicated to your private passions. Name your hobbies and special interests outside of commercial work. Are you a golfer, a tennis player or a musician? Could you teach any of those skills on a part-time basis? Or is there a product or service that you might create to service a need that you've seen when you pursued your hobby?

This is a creative exercise. You need the time and space to imagine revenue streams that could come from the potential jobs that you've listed. It's useful to consider where you'd like to be in five or ten years time (as you did in Chapter 5), and what your financial needs might be. What work would bring you fulfilment? How would you do it?

GO FOR THE SURE THING – THEN EXPAND

Having made your decision, put your plan into action by securing one job that you know you can do well. You might ask for a part-time position with your current employer. Or perhaps there are clients you can approach who don't need a full-time consultant. In any event, try to have one tent-pole job that you're certain will bring consistent revenue. That's the confidence-builder that will enable you to start your portfolio. You can grow it from there.

YES, IT'S A RISKY BUSINESS

As with self-employment in general, there is risk attached. You may lose an important client at the last minute, or the local authority that employs you in a part-time job decides to make cutbacks. There are no guarantees that you will have the same income every month. But just as wise investors have a broad investment portfolio – never putting all their eggs in one basket – you will have the advantage of spreading your risk across your job portfolio. That's something that a self-employed interim or consultant is less able to do.

There's risk in permanent, mainstream employment as well. We've seen several people come through the Job Club, find re-employment and then return to the club a year or more later when they've been made redundant – yet again. Our economy is changing and there is less certainty all around. Having a variety of income streams can protect you against uncertainty, because it is a flexible approach that allows you to pick up another part-time job should one fall out of your portfolio.

RISK HAS ITS REWARDS

Here's a short list of the benefits of a portfolio career.

- Freedom: you're in charge of your own work life.
- Enjoyment in doing what you like best.
- Flexible security: if one job goes away, you can replace it with another.
- Improvement of your motivated skills: you get better at what you do best.
- Expanded networking opportunities: more jobs means meeting more people.
- Your income is self-generating.

PRACTICAL ASPECTS

There are other things to consider in this type of career.

1. The complexities of PAYE jobs combined with contract and self-employed work are best handled by someone with expertise so you'll need an understanding accountant.
2. You will be creating multiple personas, and so you may need separate business cards and websites for each occupation in your portfolio.
3. Time management is an issue.
4. Is there synergy within your portfolio? Is the whole greater than the sum of the parts?
5. How will your clients perceive you, if they know that you do everything part-time?
6. Consider your long-term career goals. How will this look on your CV if you plan on returning to a single-track or serial career?

YOU'LL HAVE LOTS OF COMPANY

There isn't a great deal of research on the topic, but a recent estimate[8] puts the number of portfolio workers in the UK at well over 1 million, and growing. Anecdotal evidence would indicate that the number is much larger. The Office of National Statistics doesn't measure this type of employment: jobs are full- or part-time, employed or self-employed. But if we consider that there are 6.6 million part-time workers in employment, and 1 million self-employed part-time, then numbers that combine these two categories could total much more than a million.

SUMMARY

A portfolio career has now become a respectable option, one that suits many older workers. Those who enjoy multitasking and have a variety of interests are best-suited to this type of career.

Start by building on your strengths; use a cornerstone occupation – one that you enjoy doing and you know will bring revenue – as the foundation of your portfolio. Expand further and be sure to include your hobbies and special interests. What you may sacrifice in terms of security can be balanced by the satisfaction that you get from using all of your talents. Whether you set out to create a portfolio before leaving employment, or if you have it thrust upon you due to circumstance, approach it with the same care and enthusiasm that you would have devoted to your previous, single-track career. This time, you'll be in charge.

SUCCESS STORY: JUDITH WATTS

If someone had told Judith Watts at the age of 43 that she was going to be a teacher – and still enjoying it at 48 – she would have laughed at the idea. And yet that's what she's doing now. Her career journey led her to a vacancy at a university where she discovered that she had the right background and skills for a position that suits her perfectly. Judith says it didn't happen overnight; it took five years from the time she took her first tentative steps on a creative writing course. But now she says she's really looking forward to the next 20 years of her working life, with further development of her portfolio career.

Judith got her degree in English Literature at York University. Her first job after graduation was managing a bar in Manchester but she soon moved on to starting a business, using enterprise grants. It was 1982, and the company supplied healthy snacks to theatres and cinemas in London. The business didn't last, but this early initiative illustrates that Judith has an entre-preneurial streak – something of benefit to those who develop a portfolio.

She next took a job selling books at Blackwell's in Oxford and then she applied for a job in Blackwell Publishing. Judith enjoyed her first role as publicity controller, and she decided to set out on a career in publishing. Two years later, she had a job in London with Routledge. She started as a marketing assistant, worked her way up, and over the course of ten years rose to a senior marketing manager position, leading a team of 30. She says she really enjoyed the work as it put her at the leading edge in publishing: helping to develop new products and introducing them to the international market – especially the US and Asia.

Her first child was born in 1994 and Judith's job in central London became difficult to manage, so she left. In 1999, she embarked on a two-year stint with a business start-up, offering marketing and training services to the publishing industry. By the time her third child arrived in 2001, she found that a traditional approach to work was becoming impossible. She took a break, one that lasted two years. That was when panic set in: she would need income in the future and she wanted a career plan but she was indecisive about what action to take. She couldn't decide if she should develop her interest in interior design, or take up writing – something she had explored previously by studying journalism. To aid in her decision, she took a self-development course where 'I learned to stop panicking and be positive about the future,' she says. Judith decided to do something she believed in, rather than worry about money. She signed up to a local education poetry course, and enjoyed it so much that she went on to apply for an MA in Creative Writing at Kingston University. Two years later, she had her degree.

While she was studying, Kingston University was growing its publishing degree. One of Judith's instructors suggested she apply for a lectureship. She got the position because she was able to demonstrate a high level of talent, passion and commitment and she was recognised for her previous experience in the publishing industry. Those with experience in the commercial world are valued by universities if they have practical knowledge that can attract students (see Pippa's story on p.122).

Now she occupies a niche where all of her previous experience and skills are valuable. Her advice to those who might be at a similar career crossroads:

- choose something that you're really interested in and passionate about;
- be prepared to work hard at being a beginner;
- don't overthink and bring in doubts – take the plunge;
- consider that your choice is not an indulgence;
- invest in yourself;
- persevere (because it won't be easy).

The teaching role is part-time, which gives her the opportunity to do other things. She's carrying on with an MFA (she may go further and get a PhD) and she is able to perform and promote poetry at local events. It's possible that she'll start a small press.

As a summary, we can say that her years in publishing gave her the career capital that she needed to acquire the teaching role, and she's been able to combine that with her natural creativity to begin a fulfilling portfolio career.

RESOURCES

Some books referenced below may appear in more recent editions than those cited.

INTRODUCTION

The Foundation for Jobseekers (formerly the Thames Valley Executive Job Club Network) is a network of five executive job clubs in the Thames Valley. The clubs assist experienced managers who want to remain economically active, often following redundancy. Each of the executive job clubs is run by volunteers with experience of both management and redundancy.
www.tvexecutivejobclubs.org.uk

The Job Clubs
Aylesbury Careers Springboard
www.careersspringboardaylesbury.org.uk
Sivatech Ltd
Gatehouse Close
Aylesbury
Bucks HP19 8DJ
Meets on a Thursday evening (see website for details).

Gerrards Cross Careers Springboard
www.careersspringboard.info
United Reform Church Hall
Packhorse Road
Gerrards Cross SL9 7QE
Meets on a Monday evening (see website for details).

Bracknell Careers Springboard
www.careersspringboardbracknell.org.uk
Open Learning Centre
Brakenhale School
Rectory Lane
Bracknell RG12 7GR
Meets on a Friday afternoon (see website for details).

West Berkshire Careers Springboard
www.careerswestberks.org.uk
Town Hall
Mansion Street
Newbury RG14 5AA
Meets on a Tuesday afternoon (see website for details).

Windsor and Maidenhead Executive Job Club
www.executivejobclub.org.uk
The Old Vic
St Mary's Church
St Mary's Close
14 High Street
Maidenhead SL6 1YY
and
The Parish and Garrison Church of the Holy Trinity
Trinity Place
Windsor SL4 3BB
Meets on a Thursday morning in either Windsor or Maidenhead
(see website for details).

Chapter 1: The Age Factor

The Centre for Research into the Older Workforce (CROW) carries out research into the nature of the older workforce. It examines older peoples' attitudes to and experience of work, employers' responses to ageing, and policy issues that arise as the government seeks to encourage people to stay in work later in life.
www.niace.org.uk/crow

The National Institute of Adult Continuing Education (NIACE) aims to encourage all adults to engage in learning of every sort.
www.niace.org.uk

TAEN (The Age and Employment Network) works to promote an effective labour market that serves the needs of people in mid- and later life, employers and the economy.
www.taen.org.uk

Books
Hallpike, Helen. *Career Crunch!* 1st ed. London: Lulu Enterprises Inc., 2010.
www.career-crunch.com

Chapter 2: Coping with Redundancy

Jobcentre Plus, part of the UK Department for Work and Pensions, provides an online facility for searching for jobs, career information, voluntary work and childcare providers. The jobseekers web page has a wealth of information on careers, preparing for interviews, CV writing, career change etc.
www.jobseekers.direct.gov.uk

GB Job Clubs is a charity that provides training, resources and a network for job clubs.
www.gbjobclubs.org

Career consultants

There are many companies offering personalised career and job search advice for a fee. These are some we know of personally. By listing them here we do not vouch for them or recommend their services for everyone – their suitability will depend on your needs and personal circumstances.

PCS Executives: **www.pcsexecutive.com**
Proteus Career Consultancy: **www.proteusconsultancy.com**
Connaught Executive: **www.connaughtexec.com**
HDA: **www.hda.co.uk**

Volunteering

The following organisations match volunteers with open positions for volunteers.

www.do-it.org.uk
www.volunteering.org.uk
www.reachskills.org.uk

Books

Kübler-Ross, Elizabeth, and David Kessler. *On Grief and Grieving: Finding the Meaning of Grief Through the Five Stages of Loss.* London: Simon & Schuster, 2005. Kübler-Ross first presented her theory on the five stages of grief in her book *On Death and Dying* (1969).

Chapter 3: Motivate Yourself

Neuro-Linguistic Programming (NLP)

Many of the tools and techniques in this chapter are NLP based. Liam undertook his NLP training with Pegasus NLP (www.nlp-now.co.uk) and they have some useful NLP resources.

www.nlp-now.co.uk/tips-n-tech.htm

Books

Maslow, Abraham H. *Motivation and Personality.* 3rd revised ed. Hong Kong: Longman Asia Ltd, 1989.

Burton, Kate and Brinley Platts. *Building Self-Confidence for Dummies.* London: John Wiley and Sons, 2005.

Ingham, Christine. *101 Ways To Motivate Yourself.* London: Kogan Page, 2007.

Chapter 4: Self-Assessment

Alison Fair contributed the content for the section on 'skills and abilities'. She is a careers counsellor based in Maidenhead, Berkshire. You can see her profile on LinkedIn if you are a member. You can also contact Alison by e-mail: **alisonfairconsulting@yahoo.co.uk**

The Myers & Briggs Foundation is a useful first port of call if you are considering taking an online personality indicator. The website has links to accredited providers and information on results.
www.myersbriggs.org

Thomas International provides behavioural and personality tests based on the DISC model.
www.thomasinternational.net

Books

Schein, Edgar H. *Career Anchors: Discovering Your Real Values.* Revised ed. New Jersey: Jossey-Bass, 1985.
Tieger, Paul D., and Barbara Barron-Tieger. *Do What You are: Discover the Perfect Career for You Through the Secrets of Personality Type.* 3rd ed. London: Little, Brown & Company, 2001.

Chapter 5: Create a Winning Strategy

Adult Directions, from Cascaid, Loughborough University, is a unique online resource which helps adults to make decisions about their career direction. It uses your work-related interests, skills and desired occupation level to identify suitable careers.
www.cascaid.co.uk

Next Step is a publicly funded service that helps adults find the advice they need for future skills, careers, work and life choices.
https://nextstep.direct.gov.uk

Books

Covey, Stephen R. *The Seven Habits of Highly Effective People: Powerful Lessons in Personal Change.* Revised ed. London: Simon & Schuster UK Ltd, 1999.

Chapter 7: Networking or Not Working

LinkedIn is the networking site for managers and professionals with over 80 million registered users, over 11 million of which are in Europe (source: Wikipedia). If you are new to LinkedIn be sure to read the guide (http://learn.linkedin.com) or get someone at a job club to show you how it's done.
www.linkedin.com

Facebook is now the world's most popular social networking site.
www.facebook.com

Twitter is used for instant communication via short 'tweets', which are like mini-blogs. Useful if you can find the right 'streams' and, if you contribute your own tweets, it's a way of networking in social and business circles.
http://twitter.com

Ecademy is a membership organisation for entrepreneurs and business owners.
www.ecademy.com

Toastmasters is a useful club to develop your networking and communications skills while improving your ability to speak in public. Find and join a club near you at:
www.toastmasters.org

Local networking

In the UK, the following organisations run business networking groups on a local basis. They will allow you to visit and try before joining. In some cases you will need an invitation from an existing member. We do not recommend any particular event or group but list them here for you to contact.

4Networking:	**www.4networking.biz**
BNI:	**www.bni-europe.com/uk**
Refer-On:	**www.refer-on.com**
NRG:	**www.nrg-networks.com**
Business Biscotti:	**www.businessbiscotti.co.uk**
Ladies who Latte:	**www.ladieswholatte.com**
Local Chambers of Commerce:	**www.britishchambers.org.uk**
Federation of Small Business:	**www.fsb.org.uk**

Business cards

From simple to bespoke designs, effective business cards to use at your networking meetings are available at:

www.goodprint.co.uk

www.moo.com

Chapter 8: Upgrade Your Skills

UK government adult-learning gateway.

www.direct.gov.uk/en/EducationAndLearning/AdultLearning/ index.htm

The Open University: **www3.open.ac.uk**

APMG: the UK accrediting body for project management and IT service management training organisations.

www.apmg-international.com

Chapter 9: How to Find a Job

Companies House is the foundation of company information exchange in the UK. You can use their website to research companies you would like to approach.

www.companieshouse.gov.uk

Below is a selection of job sites that we have used or have had recommended to us:

Executive Grapevine: originally a database of head-hunters, this is now also a jobs board.
www.askgrapevine.com

Exec-Appointment.com: The Financial Times jobs board, 'the global job board for executives in all sectors'.
www.exec-appointments.com

The Ladders: job board for £50k+ jobs.
www.theladders.co.uk

Jobsite: **www.jobsite.co.uk**

CV Library: **www.cv-library.co.uk**

Career Site Advisor: aggregator of job sites by category and career advice.
www.careersiteadvisor.com

Indeed: job site search engine.
www.indeed.co.uk

Executives on the Web: the No. 1 UK executive jobs and career site offering free access to pre-screened senior management jobs across all industry sectors in the UK/EMEA.
www.executivesontheweb.com

Telegraph jobs board: **www.jobs.telegraph.co.uk**

Top-Consultant.com: for consultancy jobs.
www.top-consultant.com/UK/career/appointments.asp

LinkedIn jobs board: **www.linkedin.com/jobs**

Chapter 11: The Interview

GlassHouse Technologies: provides free information on salaries in industries, companies and by profession. Useful when negotiating a salary.
www.glasshouse.com

SHL: provides workplace talent assessment solutions – including ability and personality tests, and psychometric assessments.
www.shl.com

Books

Bolles , Richard N. *What Color Is Your Parachute?: A Practical Manual for Job-Hunters and Career-Changers*. Revised ed. New York: Ten Speed Press, 2010.

Fisher, Roger, and William Ury. *Getting to Yes: Negotiating an Agreement Without Giving In*. Revised 2nd ed. London: Random House Business, 2003. The classic book on negotiation.

Chapter 12: Interim Management

The Interim Management Association has lots of advice about becoming an interim, what makes a good interim, etc.
www.interimmanagement.uk.com

More advice, and information about a one-day workshop, is found on the IMA Institute website.
www.ima-institute.com

PCG (Professional Contractors Group) is an independent not-for-profit professional association that represents, supports and promotes the freelance community, with specific attention to the needs of freelancers who are members of PCG. The website also has information on setting yourself up as a freelancer.
www.pcg.org.uk

Interim agencies

The following agencies have been recommended to us by reliable sources. We do not vouch for them or recommend their services for everyone – their suitability will depend on your needs and personal circumstances. You'll find that some of them serve the public sector exclusively, while others offer services to both the private and the public sector.

Boyden	**www.boyden.com**
Gatenby Sanderson	**www.gatenbysanderson.com**
Odgers Berndtson	**www.odgersberndtson.co.uk**
Penna	**www.penna.com**
Solace	**www.solaceenterprises.com**
Tribal	**www.tribalgroup.com**
Veredus	**www.veredus.co.uk**
Your Choice Interims	**www.yourchoiceinterims.com**

Chapter 13: Consultancy

Top-Consultant.com is the leading management consultancy recruitment website in the world.
www.top-consultant.com

Skillfair is an independent online resource and network that specialises in matching small businesses and freelance consultants to projects.
www.skillfair.co.uk

Chapter 14: Start Your Own Business

Information and advice

The PRIME Initiative provides free information, events and training to help older people (over 50) get back into work by starting their own business.
www.primeinitiative.co.uk

PRIME has another website with practical information for older entrepreneurs. **www.primebusinessclub.com**

Business Link is a free nationwide (UK) business advice and support service, available online and through local advisers. **www.businesslink.gov.uk**

Startups is the UK's leading website for information and advice on starting or running a small business. **www.startups.co.uk**

Growing Business is a magazine for entrepreneurs with a useful website. **www.growingbusiness.co.uk**

Yoodoo takes you through steps in developing a business idea by using online video instruction and interactive exercises. It's free. **www.yoodoo.biz**

Company, trademark, and domain registration
Complete Formations provides information and enables company registration. **www.completeformations.co.uk**

The Company Merchant offers a similar service. **www.thecompanymerchant.co.uk**

Patent Office/Trade Marks Registry: **www.ipo.gov.uk**
Registering a domain name: **www.easily.co.uk**
Another service is: **www.123-reg.co.uk**

Angel investment
British Business Angels Association (BBAA) website is a good source of general information and a way to find an angel network near you. **www.bbaa.org.uk**

London Business Angels: **www.lbangels.co.uk**

Other funding sources

J4B is a comprehensive grants information database.
www.j4b.co.uk

The National Endowment for Science, Technology and the Arts (NESTA) provides funding and mentoring.
www.nesta.org.uk

Oxford Innovation Ltd supports the exploitation and development of science and technology, and runs investment networks.
www.oxin.co.uk

Books

Khedair, Jane and Michael Anderson. *Successful Business Plans: Get Brilliant Results Fast.* Richmond, Surrey: Crimson Publishing, 2009. Highly recommended. Michael Anderson writes from the perspective of someone who has been a successful business angel and an entrepreneur. He is a Director of Business Plan Services, a leading resource for business planning in the UK.

Southon, Mike and Chris West. *The Beermat Entrepreneur: Turn Your Good Idea into a Great Business.* 2nd ed. London: Prentice Hall, 2005. The Beermat series also includes excellent books on sales, marketing and finance. All of them are useful guides for entrepreneurs.

Gerber, Michael E. *The E-myth Revisited: Why Most Small Businesses Don't Work and What to Do About It.* 3rd revised ed. New York: HarperCollins, 2001. This is worth reading as a precautionary measure.

Chapter 15: Portfolio Career

Portfolio Professionals offers more information on the topic.
www.portfolioprofessionals.org

Portfolio Careers has a regular blog on the subject.
http://portfoliocareers.net

Books

Bourne, Adrian, Colin McCrudden and Christopher Lyons. *Building a Portfolio Career: How to Create a Portfolio of Roles to Suit Your Work and Life.* 2nd ed. Kemble: Management Books, 2009.

Hopson, Barrie, and Katie Ledger. *And What do You Do?: 10 Steps to Creating a Portfolio Career.* London: A & C Black, 2009.

NOTES

Chapter 1

1 *SERFA Conference: Summary of Skills and Employment Workshop*, 10 March 2009.

2 *ONS Labour Market Statistics*, November 2009.

3 Interview with Isabella Kerr, 16 July, 2010.

4 Cattell, R. B. *Intelligence: Its structure, growth, and action.* New York: Elsevier Science, 1987.

5 Cavanaugh, J. C., and F. Blanchard-Fields. *Adult Development and Aging.* 5th ed. Belmont, CA: Wadsworth Publishing/Thomson Learning, 2006.

6 Department for Business Innovation and Skills, *Statistical Press Release,* corrected July 2010, http://stats.bis.gov.uk/ed/sme/Stats

7 In July 2010, the government announced that it was phasing out the Default Retirement Age, beginning in April 2011.

8 Interview with Chris Ball, TAEN, 8 September, 2010.

9 Hallpike, Helen. *Career Crunch!* 1st ed. p.41. London: Lulu Enterprises Inc., 2010.

10 *The Silver Tsunami,* The Economist, 4 February, 2010.

11 Source: TAEN (The Age and Employment Network).

12 Interview with Professor Stephen McNair, 13 September 2010. At the time of writing, McNair was formally retired, but he retains his positions as Senior Research Associate at NIACE, President of the National Association of Adult Guidance, and he is a member of the UK Advisory Forum on Age.

Chapter 2

1   Kübler-Ross, Elizabeth, and David Kessler. *On Grief and Grieving: Finding the Meaning of Grief Through the Five Stages of Loss.* London: Simon & Schuster, 2005. Kübler-Ross first presented her theory on the five stages of grief in her book *On Death and Dying* (1969).

2   http://en.wikipedia.org/wiki/Elizabeth_Kübler-Ross

Chapter 3

1   *The Concise Oxford Dictionary*, 7th ed. Oxford: Clarendon Press.

2   Maslow, Abraham H. *Motivation and Personality.* New York: Harper, 1954.

3   Carroll, Lewis. *Alice's Adventures in Wonderland.*

Chapter 4

1   http://uk.linkedin.com/pub/alison-fair/4/69/386

2   Schein, Edgar H, *Career Anchors: Discovering Your Real Values,* Jossey-Bass: Revised edition, 1985

3   Isabel Briggs Myers introduced the concept of four dimensions to assess personality: I (Introverted) or E(Extroverted), S(Sensing) or N (Intuitive), T (Thinking) or F (Feeling), P (Perceptive) or J (Judging) and devised a test to determine a person's preference. This is now known widely as the Myers-Briggs Personality Indicator (MBTI). A person who 'is ISTJ' tends to have preferences for Introvert Sensing Thinking Judging.

4   Proteus Consultancy, www.proteusconsultancy.com

5   http://www.cascaid.co.uk/home/main.do?section_id=373)

6   Tieger, Paul D., and Barbara Barron-Tieger. *Do What You are: Discover the Perfect Career for You Through the Secrets of Personality Type.* 3rd ed. Little, Brown & Company, 2001.

Chapter 5

1   Covey, Stephen R., *The Seven Habits of Highly Effective People: Powerful Lessons in Personal Change.* Revised ed. London: Simon & Schuster UK Ltd, 1999.

Chapter 7

1   Based on a method of categorising business contacts according to usefulness in personal effectiveness courses run by Leadership Management International (LMI).

Chapter 10

1   ONS Statistical Bulletin, Public Sector Employment, 16 September 2009.

Chapter 11

1   Bolles, Richard N. *What is Your Parachute?: A Practical Manual for Job-Hunters and Career Changers*. Revised ed. New York: Ten Speed Press, 2010.

Chapter 14

1   *South East 40-70 Tomorrows Workforce Programme, Interim Report*: June 25, 2009.

2   Source: *Business Angel Investing: A Guide to the Legal, Technical & Regulatory Issues*. Found online at: www.bbaa.org.uk/library/file/BBAA_Legal_FAQs_Single_Page_Format.pdf

3   To determine if your company is eligible for EIS tax relief, visit: www.hmrc.gov.uk/eis

4   The Silver Academy was a project designed and implemented in 2010/11 to help unemployed people over 50 to start their own business. It was a partnership between the University of Surrey and South East England Chambers of Commerce, in conjunction with the southern Spanish region of Andalusia and the Malopolska region in Poland.

Chapter 15

1   Hopson, Dr Barrie. *From Vocational Guidance to Portfolio Careers: A Critical Reflection*. 12th Annual Lecture, University of Derby, 10th December 2009.
www.derby.ac.uk/files/icegs_from_vocational_guidance_to_portfolio_careers.pdf

2   Handy, Charles. *The Age of Unreason*. London: Hutchinson, 1989.

3   Bourne, Adrian, Colin McCrudden and Christopher Lyons, *Building a Portfolio Career*. p.38 Cirencester: Management Books 2000 Ltd, 2009.

4   *www.globalideasbank.org/site/bank/idea.php?ideaId=1100*

5   Hopson, Barrie, and Katie Ledger. *And What Do You Do?: 10 Steps to Creating a Portfolio Career*. London: A & C Black, 2009.

6   Hopson, Dr Barrie, vocational guidance speech as above.

7   Bourne, et al. p. 180.

8   These are the 1.13 million workers described by the Office of National Statistics (August, 2010) as: 'workers with second jobs'.

INDEX